Hey Buddy!

Welcome! I'll be your Catalyst Guide. Let's get started!

— Megan

WHAT PEOPLE ARE SAYING ABOUT MEGAN

&

DISCOVER. ACT. ENGAGE.

"*Discover. Act. Engage.* is motivating, thought-provoking, inspiring, and highly recommended!"

— **Kathleen Tucker,** Leadership Education Conference Coordinator, Alpha Chi Omega

"Megan delivered an engaging presentation which got her audience involved and stretched their thinking. Her style is very dynamic and her message is spot-on! Megan is a pleasure to learn from and you will leave with take-away tools that you can apply immediately to help you achieve your goals."

— **Susan Young,** Speaker & Author, Susan Young International

"Megan grabs your attention, actively engages you during the activities, and empowers you to pursue your dreams without fear."

— **Jon Cleveland,** Assistant Director for Career Education, University of Wisconsin-Madison

"Megan was really great and humorous! Loved the interactive activities, especially the networking one. Inspiring personal stories too."

— **Sarah Gang,** Student, UW-La Crosse

"Organized, yet relaxed and relatable. Applicable to all age groups."

— **Elisabeth Caldwell,** Intern, Dream Bank

"LOVE THE MESSAGE, YOUR CONFIDENCE, THE MESSAGE!!!!!! I am sort of the dork on the edge of my seat, listening, learning, and being inspired all at the same time! Thanks for continuing to "grow" my inner Spark to aspire to better things!"

— **John Sayre,** Casualty Claims Adjuster, American Family Insurance

"Interactive, fun! Megan was very energetic, relatable, and encouraging. I learned the power of writing down my goals!"

— **Libbi Chapin,** Student, UW-Oshkosh

"Strong examples with specifics. Easy to use tools – easy to follow up on and execute."

— **Jenie Gao,** Professional Artist, Jenie Gao Studio

"Relatable, practical knowledge shared which can be put to use immediately."

— **Carolyn Whittaker,** Development & Training Manager, MGE

"Learned a lot about confidence and believing in myself. Megan really captures attention and holds it the whole time."

— **Katherine Zettel,** Student, Career Kickstart Program

"*Discover. Act. Engage.* brought students out and got them participating actively in exploring their dreams while taking the initiative to get started on making those dreams happen. Students are still talking about this program and what they took away from it."

— **Richard Baker,** Residence Hall Coordinator, University of Wisconsin-Madison

Discover.
Act.
Engage.

A 60-Day Catalyst Guide to
Accomplishing Your
Someday Goals!

MEGAN WATT

Important Disclaimer

This publication contains material for educational purposes only. The author and publisher have made every effort to ensure that the information in this book was correct at press time. The author and publisher do not assume and hereby disclaim any liability to any party for any loss, damage, or disruption caused by errors or omissions, whether such errors or omissions result from negligence, accident, or any other cause. The advice and strategies contained herein may not be suitable for every situation. This work is sold with the understanding that the Author and the Publisher are not engaged in rendering legal, accounting, or other professional services. Neither the Author nor the Publisher shall be liable for damages arising here from. The fact that an organization or website is referred to in this work as a citation or a potential source of further information does not mean that the Author or Publisher endorses the information that the organization or website may provide or recommendations it may make.

ISBN-13 978-0692678527
ISBN-10 0692678522
Cover Design by justdigitalinc.com
Editing by Ryan-Ashley Anderson, ryanashleyanderson.com

HELP OTHERS ACCOMPLISH THEIR *SOMEDAY GOALS!*

Share this book with your friends, family, and colleagues.

Special discounts are available on quantity purchases by corporations, associations, and others.

- Buy 25 copies and receive a 25% discount off the retail price.

- Buy 50 copies or more and receive a 50% discount off the retail price.

To place an order, contact the publisher at:

Dream Catalyst Publications
29 S. Walbridge Ave., Suite A, Madison, WI 53714
(850) 591-9449
dreamcatalyst.org

A SPECIAL INVITATION

FREE Bonus Gift for YOU!

To help you achieve your **Someday Goals,** I've included a TON of FREE Resources for you at:

DiscoverActEngage.com

Resources include templates, examples, and all of the tools I mention in the book – I utilize all these in my own life and business to help me accomplish my **Someday Goals**.

Visit **DiscoverActEngage.com** to stay connected with the *Discover. Act. Engage.* community and connect with like-minded individuals who are already taking action toward their **Someday Goals.** Together, we will design the future of the community!

If you would like to connect with me personally on social media, follow me on Twitter @megwatt or connect with me on LinkedIn at Linkedin.com/in/meganwatt

DEDICATION

For Ilsa.

You make me a better person and the world a better place.

And to Mama Watt and my grandparents (John & Patricia Watt) for your unconditional love and support. None of this would be possible without you.

TABLE OF CONTENTS

Discover. Act. Engage.

THE JOURNEY OF THE CATALYST GUIDE

I can't believe I'm sitting here writing this sentence. I'm 30,000 feet high in the air, the guy sitting next to me is sleeping, and here I am, writing the introduction to my FIRST book!!! Yes, it's a first book, and everyone who writes is excited about this moment, but it's particularly momentous for me.

I've never considered myself a reader or a writer. It's only been in the last few years that I've even found reading enjoyable. Writing papers in grad school was a painful task I always put off until the last minute, which just exacerbated my anxiety, making the experience that much more excruciating. There's nothing worse than being crunched for time on a task you dread. In hindsight, that time crunch 'training' really helped me get to where I am today.

You see, a week ago I was talking to a very good friend of mine about how I could provide more value to my audience by offering expanded services. I was fixated on the idea of figuring out some way people could take me home with them...well, maybe not me, but my message!

The mission of my company, Dream Catalyst Labs, is to inspire people to go after their *Someday Goals*. I believe people who dare to dream and play to their greatest strengths can make a real difference and change the world. There's a 'why' behind every mission, and that one is mine. Helping people find their strengths and achieve their goals is the entire reason I do what I do.

One of the ways I enact my 'why' statement and grow my company's mission is by making sure the knowledge we share has a lasting effect.

As an instructor, I made a promise to myself and to my students that I would never be a traditional "sit-n-git" lecturer. My classes and my programs are ALWAYS experiential, borrowing ideas from the Socratic teaching method. My colleagues and I know that information is better received when you engage with the content. Studies have shown you just don't retain as much when you're only utilizing your listening skills for long periods of time.

I've digressed a little, but now you understand a little more about my teaching background, style, and beliefs. Now, back to why this is book is such a surprise.

Remember that conversation I mentioned having about finding a way to provide my audience with take-home material that would allow them to keep learning? The conversation led to the idea of creating a more in-depth activity workbook to correlate with my #1 Keynote, *Discover. Act. Engage.*

I knew I had dozens more activities and exercises than what I could fit in a 60 minute keynote, so the Saturday after that brainstorming conversation, I did a mind map related to each phase of *Discover. Act. Engage.* – a method one of my Dream Team members, Adam Carroll taught me for content creation – and in 30 minutes, I had developed the bones for 90 activities. I stopped there, because 90 seemed like the perfect number for a workbook.

The next day, Sunday, I created an outline, talked to one of my colleagues from Dream Catalyst Labs' Board of Directors, and cut the activities to 20 per phase. By Monday, I had begun diving into the writing process. Because I had prepared by mapping everything out, the words just flew onto the screen.

I was 100% geeked out about everything I was writing because it's all stuff I'm extremely passionate about and love teaching, so I just wrote and wrote and wrote. Using the Pomodoro Technique (more on this later), I was able to stay incredibly focused while avoiding burnout. On Tuesday, I wrote for a few hours in the morning and found an editor through a friend of mine. I talk a lot about maintaining connections and this is a perfect example of what can happen when you maintain and seek out meaningful connections – people want to find a way to help you, either by being of service or making introductions! I wrote a little bit more that day and then sent the first 20 Challenges over to my editor.

Sometime between Sunday and Tuesday, I realized that one of my goals with this workbook was to help people **take action** toward a ***Someday Goal***, and that creating Challenges was going to be the best way to do that, so the workbook format transitioned into what you see now, a Catalyst Guide.

Now it's Wednesday, and not even a week has gone by. I'm not sure what was in the air that day, or what happened during my Miracle Morning routine (more on this later too), but I was in the zone! I wrote all day and pumped out over 6,000 words! With the added *Catalyst Moves*, my challenges were becoming more rich – they became filled with specific tools for really helping you jumpstart your project for the first time or catapult goals to the next level. I also added *Watt's Lightbulb Moments* which include personal insights and mega key points.

When I realized I was at 8,000 words with 15 Challenges to go, I had a very important *Watt's Lightbulb Moment* of my own – this "little" activity workbook had morphed into a real book disguised as a Catalyst Guide!

Thursday came and I finished the book by late afternoon (approximately 4:53 CST if you really want to know). I was DONE!!! I was Over 13,000 words! I couldn't believe it. It felt like I had begun going through the stages of grief, a common experience when coming to the end of a big project.

First, I stared at the screen in shock for a while. Then, I got up and walk aimlessly around my office for a few minutes as denial was replaced by the reality of all the work I had just done. Finally, I came to acceptance. "OMG, I just wrote a book, and I did it in only 4 days!!"

Mama Watt, please don't worry. I was still getting plenty of sleep during those four days. No matter what, moms will always worry, and mine is no exception!

It's Friday afternoon and almost a week has gone by. I'm on my way to a dear friend's surprise birthday party, and I'm writing the introduction to my first book. I'm shocked, excited, nervous, happy, and most of all, proud. Life's a journey and mine has been a FUN one so far, filled with lots of twists and turns.

Writing this book was never a turn I thought I would take, but it has been the most delightful detour. To be exact, I'm "super pumped" about it! My journey is evidence that with the right mentors, commitment to the goal, utilizing time management tools, and relying on my network, I was able to knock one more thing off my bucket list, all while managing to get a full night's sleep (or really close it), every night.

If you made it this far into my introduction, THANK YOU so much. I hope this book inspires you to begin pursuing and accomplishing your **Someday Goals** today. I guarantee you, it's within reach. No matter what your **Someday Goal** is – reducing debt and buying a house; going back to school; landing your dream job; writing your first book – I know this book is going to help you, because the things I'm writing about have already helped me and so many others achieve **Someday Goals**!

The best part is, you don't have to do this alone. Within, you'll find 60-Days' worth of Challenges designed to help guide you every step of the way. Whether you're ready to dive right in or feel more comfortable taking some time to test the water, this is a custom experience, tailored to fit every personality and work style. Complete the book in 60 days, or spread it out. Go in order, or mix it up. No matter how you use your Catalyst Guide, you're guaranteed to start visualizing your **Someday Goals** in no time.

I'm honored you've chosen me and my team to be your guide to achieving your **Someday Goals**. Cheers, and good luck!

Your guide,

Megan Watt

Discover.

How to discover your **Someday Goals**, your ideal day, and who you are both now and in the future.

"The future belongs to those who believe in the beauty of their DREAMS."

— Eleanor Roosevelt

1. *SOMEDAY GOAL* VISUALIZATION

Visualization is such a powerful tool – some even call it a secret weapon. From Olympic Gold medalists Michael Phelps and Lindsey Vonn, to actors like Jim Carrey and Will Smith, and even Oprah Winfrey, they all credit their ability to accomplish BIG goals to *visualization.*

> **Your Challenge**: Draw or write down the *Someday Goal* you visualized during the *Discover. Act. Engage.* keynote. If you haven't had the chance to experience this powerful visualization exercise yet, head over to **discoveractengage.com** and listen to it!

My goal is to become a therapist.
I see myself sitting down in a chair in my own office as they come in

2. YOUR IDEAL DAY

Your ideal day may seem like something that could only exist in a Neverland dream world, but there is real power in what you put out into the universe, including what you visualize. Jack Canfield's book, *The Success Principles*, featured the following brilliant exercise:

Imagine your typical ideal day. This isn't supposed to be all sandy beaches and snow-capped mountains, but instead, just a lovely, average day. It could be hanging out at the beach, or it could be a great day of work filled with accomplishments.

> **Your Challenge**: Visualize every part of your ideal day, from waking up to falling asleep at night. It should include even the little things, like your morning routine.

- What would your ideal day look like?
- What time did you wake up?
- How are you feeling? Healthy, excited, calm, stress free?
- What do you eat for breakfast?
- What does your environment look like?
- What are you wearing?
- What work do you do?
- Who are you hanging out with?
- What do you have for lunch?
- What does the evening look like (something planned or is it a relaxing evening in)?
- What does your bedtime routine look like?

Use these prompts as you visualize your ideal day. Write about what you saw on the next page.

Megan Watt

3. CHARACTERISTICS OF YOUR IDEAL/ DREAM JOB

Think about an ideal/dream job. For many of us, we can't pinpoint exactly what our ideal/dream job is, and details like what our roles, titles, or even what our field of work would be, are elusive. That's ok! You can think about some of the key characteristics you want in this ideal/dream job. And that's exactly what you're going to do now!

> **Your Challenge**: Write down all of the characteristics about your ideal/dream job that you can imagine: (this may include who you interact with, your environment, how it makes you feel, etc.)

_____

_____

_____

_____

_____

_____

_____

_____

_____

4. BACK TO THE FUTURE...OF YOU!

I tend to be someone who lives in the here and now, and in the past, I rarely thought about the future without being prompted. But I've got news for you – you *can* teach an old dog new tricks! After digesting dozens of personal development books, podcasts, and articles about success, goals, and change, I've realized how important it is to look into the future. You need to have some sort of target within sight so you know what you are aiming toward.

> **Your Challenge**: Imagine yourself 20 years from now. What do you look like? How old will you be? Now I want you to identify at least 10 characteristics that describe this future version of yourself.

_____   _____

_____   _____

_____   _____

_____   _____

_____   _____

_____   _____

_____   _____

_____   _____

_____   _____

5. BUCKET LIST

You've probably heard of bucket lists, but just in case you haven't, it's a list of things you want to do before you...kick the proverbial bucket. There's even a great movie about it with Jack Nicholson and Morgan Freeman called *The Bucket List* and I highly recommend watching it. Anyway, now is your chance to go big and think about all of the things you want to do before you kick the bucket!

A few of mine include: Go to every Major League Baseball park, visit every continent except Antarctica, learn to surf, ~~own my own business~~ (completed as of January 2015), start a non-profit, and many more.

Your Challenge: Write your own Bucket List

_____   _____

_____   _____

_____   _____

_____   _____

_____   _____

_____   _____

_____   _____

_____   _____

6. PAIL LIST

Hopefully you filled out your bucket list on the previous page. Maybe you thought a bucket list was too overwhelming, though, and skipped ahead instead. Either way, the pail list is definitely for you. This isn't as well known a concept as 'the bucket list', but it's just as important.

A pail list is a list of things you want to do, but the things aren't as big, expensive, or far away as some of your bucket list items are. Whereas your bucket list contains the biggest of the big, the pail list should be filled with small things you want to accomplish within the next few months to a year.

A few of mine: Go to one new MLB park, visit a new state, try a new fancy restaurant in town, and read *Think and Grow Rich*.

Your Challenge: Write your own Pail List

_____   _____

_____   _____

_____   _____

_____   _____

_____   _____

_____   _____

_____   _____

_____   _____

7. THINGS YOU HATE/DREAD

Part of the ***Discover.*** process involves identifying things you like and want to do, but it's also important to discover what you don't like, and what you definitely don't want to do. Sometimes, it takes investigating wrong turns and exploring dislikes to uncover your true passions.

Your Challenge: Jot down things that you hate or dread. It can include activities, types of books, food, feelings, places, etc.

_____

_____

_____

_____

_____

_____

_____

_____

_____

_____

_____

_____

8. THINGS YOU PROCRASTINATE

We're all guilty of procrastination. Sometimes it's paying bills, and sometimes it's returning a library book. Take a few moments to think of the things or activities you tend to procrastinate most often, and list them below.

For me it's making a phone call, completing household chores, and taking time to reflect. These are a few of mine; what are some of yours?

> **Your Challenge**: Make a list of all the things or activities you procrastinate about. Go! Yes, right now!

_____

_____

_____

_____

_____

_____

_____

_____

_____

9. WHAT YOU NEVER WANT IN A JOB

In Challenge #3, you came up with a list of characteristics you WANT in your ideal/dream job. Now it's time to flip the script, and pinpoint specific characteristics you NEVER want in a job.

Your Challenge: Identify any and all of the characteristics you NEVER want to find in a job. Characteristics may include who you interact with, your environment, how it makes you feel, etc.

_____

_____

_____

_____

_____

_____

_____

_____

_____

_____

_____

10. WHO YOU'LL NEVER BE

It is sometimes easier to identify what you don't like or want than it is to describe what you do like or want. Consider what you feel like when trying to decide what to eat for dinner with friends – It's a constant back and forth of, "I'll eat anything," and, "It doesn't matter to me," and then as soon as someone finally makes a suggestion, you hear, "Well, anything except that." I sense the head nodding and ear-to-ear smiles from here because you've experienced this same dialogue.

Back in Challenge #4, you wrote about characteristics that describe yourself 20 years from now. We are going to flip the script again, and identify characteristics that you NEVER want to be described as.

Your Challenge: Make a list of at least 10 characteristics you NEVER want to be described as now, or in the future.

_____

_____

_____

_____

_____

_____

_____

_____

11. TIMES OF JOY!!

When trying to discover our dream jobs, **Someday Goals**, and our life's calling, it's important to connect with times in our lives when we truly experienced joy. When we do what we love, it should be a joyful experience.

> **Your Challenge**: Look back at your life and identify the things that brought you the greatest joy.

FROM AGE 0-10:

FROM AGE 11-19:

FROM AGE 20-29:

FROM AGE 30-39:

FROM AGE 40-49:

FROM AGE 50-59:

FROM AGE 60+:

12. YOU'RE THE AVERAGE OF THE...

Jim Rohn, one of the first thought leaders in the personal development arena said, "You are the average of the five people you spend the most time with."

My question to you is, who do you hang out with the most? Are you hanging out with dreamers, people who motivate and push you, risk takers, innovators, and people who bring you joy, or are you spending time with "Negative Nancy's/Nathan's", people who belittle you, squish dreams and passions, and settle for the status quo?

Your Challenge: List the five people you hang out with most here:

1. _____

2. _____

3. _____

4. _____

5. _____

Reflect on your list. Are they adding to or subtracting from your life's goals? The bottom line is, success begets success. Hang with driven people who strive to do good, and they'll be there to encourage and celebrate your successes.

_____

_____

_____

13. WHAT'S YOUR PERSONALITY TYPE?

Self-awareness is a key part of discovery, and an effective way to jumpstart your understanding about *anything* is to assess it. A common tool for assessing self-awareness is through identifying your personality type.

Your Challenge: Please complete the following personality assessment or download a version of it as **discoveractengage.com.**

Personality Assessment Questionnaire

- For each of the following 20 prompts choose a. or b.
- Record your answers on the score sheet below the question
- The score sheet runs horizontally along the row before going down
- Choose the answer that you think most accurately describes you
- Even if you agree with both answers, check one you agree with more
- Answer as you really are, not based on who you want to be
- Make choices for the majority of your life situations
- Having strong interests should not be used to cloud the results
- Think of situations in which you are free to be yourself
- There are no right or wrong answers
- Answer honestly

1. a. expend energy, enjoy groups	OR	b. conserve energy, enjoy one-on-one
2. a. interpret literally	OR	b. look for meaning and possibilities
3. a. logical, thinking, questioning	OR	b. empathetic, feeling, accommodating
4. a. organized, orderly	OR	b. flexible, adaptable
5. a. more outgoing, think out loud	OR	b. more reserved, think to yourself
6. a. practical, realistic, experiential	OR	b. imaginative, innovative, theoretical
7. a. candid, straight forward, frank	OR	b. tactful, kind, encouraging
8. a. plan, schedule	OR	b. unplanned, spontaneous
9. a. seek many tasks, public activities, interaction with others	OR	b. seek private, solitary activities with quiet to concentrate
10. a. standard, usual, conventional	OR	b. different, novel, unique
11. a. firm, tend to criticize, hold the line	OR	b. gentle, tend to appreciate, conciliate
12. a. regulated, structured	OR	b. easygoing, "live" and "let live"
13. a. external, communicative, express yourself	OR	b. internal, reticent, keep to yourself
14. a. focus on here-and-now	OR	b. look to the future, global perspective, "big picture"
15. a. tough-minded, just	OR	b. tender-hearted, merciful
16. a. preparation, plan ahead	OR	b. go with the flow, adapt as you go
17. a. active, initiate	OR	b. reflective, deliberate
18. a. facts, things, "what is"	OR	b. ideas, dreams, "what could be," philosophical
19. a. matter of fact, issue-oriented	OR	b. sensitive, people-oriented, compassionate
20. a. control, govern	OR	b. latitude, freedom

Record Your Answers Here:

1.		2.		3.		4.	
5.		6.		7.		8.	
9.		10.		11.		12.	
13.		14.		15.		16.	
17.		18.		19.		20.	

Score Sheet: How to Find Out Your Type

- Transfer your answers from the previous sheet to the score card below
- Total the number of marks in each column (see the example if needed)
- Put the letter with the highest number in the bottom box for each pair (if you have a tie review the description of each dichotomy or the different types – ESFP vs ENFP, and self-select the best fit

Personality Type Score Card

	a	b		a	b		a	b		a	b
1.			2.			3.			4.		
5.			6.			7.			8.		
9.			10.			11.			12.		
13.			14.			15.			16.		
17.			18.			19.			20.		
Total			**Total**			**Total**			**Total**		
	E	I		S	N		T	F		J	P

Sample Score Card

	a	b		a	b		a	b		a	b
1.	X		2.	X		3.		X	4.	X	
5.	X		6.	X		7.		X	8.		X
9.	X		10.		X	11.	X		12.		X
13.		X	14.	X		15.		X	16.		X
17.	X		18.	X		19.	X		20.		X
Total	4	1	**Total**	4	1	**Total**	2	3	**Total**	4	1
	E	I		S	N		T	F		J	P
	E			S			F			P	

Go to **discoveractengage.com** to learn more about the different personality types and associated resources.

14. VALUES

Values make up a set of beliefs that guide our decision making. Review the values listed below. Please feel free to add any values that are important to you that are not listed.

Your Challenge: Put a star next to all the values that are important to you, including any you may have added.

Achievement	Family	Influence	Respect
Adventure	Freedom	Integrity	Responsibility
Authenticity	Friendship	Justice	Service
Challenge	Fun	Knowledge	Status
Compassion	Growth	Love	Success
Creativity	Happiness	Loyalty	Wealth
Faith	Health	Peace	Wisdom
Fame	Honesty	Power	Work

Next, take 2-3 minutes to narrow the starred values down to your top 5-7 by circling the most important values.

Narrow this list of 5-7 down to your top 2 core values. Write why you hold each value so strongly. Example: Value = Service. Explanation = I think we are all meant to make the world a better place, and serving others is how I try to make an impact.

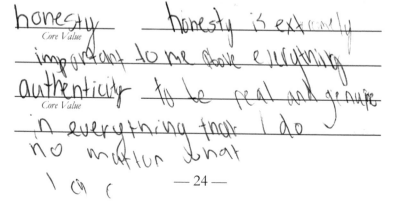

honesty
Core Value
honesty is extremely important to me above everything

authenticity
Core Value
to be real and genuine in everything that I do no matter what I am

15. STRENGTHS

I call strengths your super powers. When strengths are understood and applied, the results are unbelievable. I'm talking upwards of 800% increase. Don't take my word for it – Google "Gallup speed reading study" and see for yourself, or just come to one of my strengths programs!

One of the most effective ways to identify your strengths is to take *Gallup's StrengthsFinder assessment. You can find information about getting a code along with tons of other strengths resources at: **discoveractengage.com**

> **Your Challenge**: Take the StrengthsFinder assessment and then list your Top 5 strengths here:
>
> 1. _____
> 2. _____
> 3. _____
> 4. _____
> 5. _____

Quick Reflection: What was your initial reaction to your Top 5?

_____

_____

_____

*Note from the Author: For the record, I am not directly affiliated with Gallup nor do I get any commission from them if you take their StrengthsFinder assessment. I just love discovering strengths and believe this assessment is key. I am Gallup-trained and use the knowledge I learned with them, as well as independent research, to develop and unleash my own superpowers daily!

16. YOUR PERSONAL PROFILE

All of the Challenges until now have been designed to help you ***Discover***. Things about yourself. Now it's time to bring everything together.

> **Your Challenge**: Fill in the 4 areas of YOU (or what I like to think of as your self-awareness VIPS).

TOP 5 VALUES	INTERESTS/
1.	TIMES OF JOY
2.	
3.	
4.	
5.	

PERSONALITY	TOP 5 STRENGTHS
TYPE	1.
	2.
	3.
	4.
	5.

After filling in each of the VIPS, take a few minutes and reflect on what you see. Write about any common trends or themes. Consider how the different VIPS relate to each other.

_____

_____

_____

17. PEOPLE YOU ADMIRE

Many people throughout history have alluded to this concept, and I couldn't agree with them more. My friend, Hal Elrod, author of the best-selling book *The Miracle Morning* (p.s. more on this magical routine in the ***Act.*** section of this guide), said, "Look at other people's success to see what is possible."

Your Challenge: List the five people you admire.

1. _____

2. _____

3. _____

4. _____

5. _____

Now, briefly write about why you admire each of them:

_____

_____

_____

_____

_____

_____

_____

18. EXPLORATION OPPORTUNITIES

We receive cues throughout our life (from parents, teachers, movies, etc.) that we should have a firm plan for our future in order to be successful. I believe that a successful and meaningful life should include exploration, creativity, and play.

Additionally, trying out new things is a great way to uncover new passions and develop strengths and skills. Let's think about some ways you can seek out opportunities to explore.

Identify five exploration opportunities that would catalyze growth in your world. Consider experiences you have always wanted to have, organizations you would like to work/intern for or volunteer with, classes you could take, and skills or expertise you hope to gain.

Your Challenge: List five exploration opportunities.

1. _____
2. _____
3. _____
4. _____
5. _____

P.S. If you're struggling to think of or find exploration opportunities, jump to Challenge #20 or #60 for some help!

19. INFORMATIONAL INTERVIEWS

Now that you have identified some exploration opportunities, think about people you know who may be able to offer some help in making them happen (Challenge #23 can assist with this if you get stuck). For example, if you want to work in the music industry, you could reach out to a concert venue in your area and ask to meet with the manager to learn more about how and why they chose their job, what they like/dislike about it, and advice they have for someone aspiring to enter the field.

This process of reaching out to others who have achieved a goal or dream similar to your own and asking how they achieved it is called an informational interview. You may question why someone would be willing to meet with you, but I have learned two truths by using this process myself:

1.) People love talking about themselves.

2.) It makes people feel good to help out another person who has similar dreams and goals.

Brainstorm people who have roles or who have achieved goals you would like to meet with and learn from. Consider contacts you already know who could offer advice or connections, acquaintances of friends, family, and colleagues, or others in your community. Do some foundational research and prepare thoughtful questions in advance, so you are not asking questions easily answered via a quick Google search.

Your Challenge: Identify at least 10 people who you would want to do an informational interview with. Within the next 48 hours, reach out to at least 1 of them to arrange a meeting time.

Name: **Role/Reason You Want to Talk:**

_____   _____

_____   _____

_____   _____

_____   _____

_____   _____

_____   _____

_____   _____

_____   _____

_____   _____

_____   _____

_____   _____

_____   _____

_____   _____

_____   _____

20. EXPLORE THE WORLD OF WORK & OCCUPATIONS

By now, you have identified and explored opportunities, and have hopefully begun to talk with individuals who have experience or knowledge related to your **Someday Goal**.

Three incredible resources I want to introduce will allow you to dig deeper into a particular field or specific career, and provide opportunities for greater connections.

1. **ONETonline:** www.onetonline.org

    Search industries and occupations, and prepare to be geeked out! This site highlights job tasks, knowledge, skills, abilities needed, education or credentials required, affiliated work styles and values, and related occupations.

2. **Occupational Outlook Handbook:** www.bls.gov/ooh/

    Browse occupations by industry or projected growth rate to get ideas, or go ahead and search a specific job. This includes easy to navigate tabs with a job summary and description, information on work environment, how to achieve that job title (i.e.; experience or education needed), pay data, and hiring trends.

3. **Professional Associations:** Google [field, interest, or job title] followed by "professional association". Seriously, do it. I just searched "knitter professional association" and found The Knitting Guild Association and The National NeedleArts Association. Now I'm not about to become a professional knitter, but professional associations are a fantastic way to learn about trends in a specific field or

industry, gain access to a network of experts, and find out about educational opportunities via classes, speakers, and conferences. There is typically at least one, if not multiple professional associations or organizations for every field and industry.

Your Challenge: Explore different occupations by using one or all three of the resources. If you think you know all of the occupations, then try searching "perfusionist".

_____

_____

_____

_____

_____

_____

_____

_____

_____

_____

_____

Act.

How to break things into manageable sizes and take action in order to achieve your **Someday Goal!**

"You are 39.5% more likely to achieve a goal when write it down!"

— The ONE Thing

*Based on a study by Dr. Gail Matthews

21. GOAL SETTING FOR YOUR DREAMS

This is an exercise designed to help you break down something as huge as a **Someday Goal** into more manageable pieces. If you look at the questions below and think, "IMPOSSIBLE!" don't worry. Skip to Challenge #22 – another less daunting goal activity. If you're excited about starting in on your biggest goal, then let's dive right in.

> **Your Challenge**: Work through these questions. Usually, you start with the **Someday Goal** and work your way down. It's more than ok to skip one section and jump to the next.

Someday Goal: What's the ONE Thing I want to do someday? Go BIG and get SPECIFIC.

5 Year Goal: Based on my **Someday Goal**, what's the ONE Thing I can do in the next 5 years… such that by doing it, everything else will be easier or unnecessary?

1 Year Goal: Based on my five year goal, what's the ONE Thing I can do this year… such that by doing it, everything else will be easier or unnecessary?

Monthly Goal: Based on my one year goal, what's the ONE Thing I can do this month... such that by doing it, everything else will be easier or unnecessary?

Weekly Goal: Based on my monthly goal, what's the ONE Thing I can do this week... such that by doing it, everything else will be easier or unnecessary?

Daily Goal: Based on my weekly goal, what's the ONE Thing I can do today... such that by doing it, everything else will be easier or unnecessary?

Right Now: Based on my daily goal, what's the ONE Thing I can do right now... such that by doing it, everything else will be easier or unnecessary?

If you want to write down a clean version of this process, here's your chance:

Someday Goal: _____

↓

5 Year Goal: _____

↓

1 Year Goal: _____

↓

Monthly Goal: _____

↓

Weekly Goal: _____

↓

Daily Goal: _____

↓

Right Now: _____

*Note from the Author: The 'Goal Setting for Your Dreams' is adapted from concepts in the book, *The One Thing* by Gary Keller and Jay Papasan.

22. DREAM LADDER

Choosing a goal is half the challenge, but it can often be the most overwhelming part. Identifying the steps you need to take to achieve your goal is the other half. To help you take action, we are going to reverse engineer your goals. Whether you've heard me speak about reverse engineering or need a refresher in it, head over to **discover-actengage.com** for a short overview.

> **Your Challenge**: Write an important goal in the large oval (this could be a monthly or year goal from Challenge #21). Then, write the first step on the lowest rung of the ladder and work your way up closer to the goal. There can be five or fewer steps

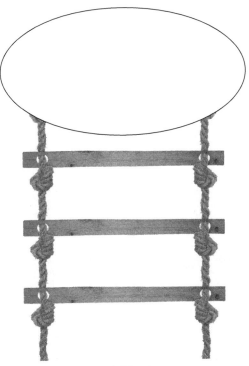

DREAM LADDER: PROFESSIONAL

Use this ladder to write about your professional dreams.

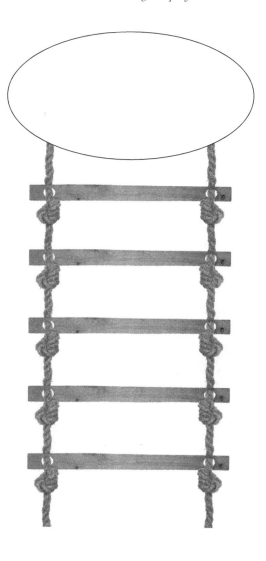

DREAM LADDER: PERSONAL

Use this ladder to write about your personal dreams.

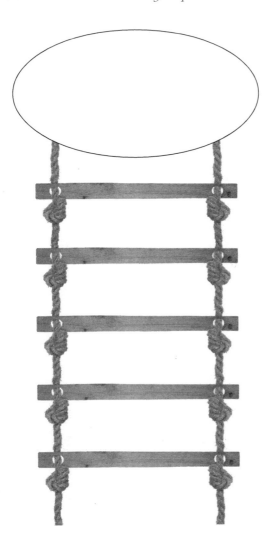

DREAM LADDER: _____

Use this ladder to write about any other kind of goal you can imagine.

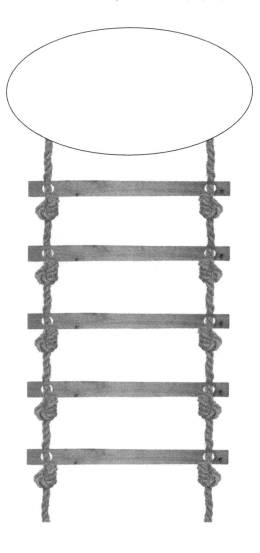

23. BUILD A DREAM TEAM

Nothing of significance has ever happened alone. All of the successful people you can think of had some help along the way. In order to accomplish a **Someday Goal**, or a mini goal on the way toward your **Someday Goal**, you need to have a "Dream Team". There are six critical categories in your Dream Team: *Cheerleaders, Industry Insiders, Connectors, Momentum Movers, Outliers, and Rising Stars.*

> **Your Challenge**: Read the definitions of each Dream Team member category below and then add people who fit into the different categories. Dream Team members may fit into multiple categories, but push to find different people for each. If you need to leave some blank, that's ok, it just means you have work to do.

Watt's Lightbulb Moment: We NEED a full Dream Team to achieve our goals!

Cheerleaders: provide encouragement/unconditional support

-
-
-
-

Industry Insiders: authorities who provide an expert lens

-
-
-
-

Connectors: super networkers willing to make intros

-
-
-
-

Momentum Movers: people who provide inspiration and push you

-
-
-
-

Outliers: people who provide a view outside your industry

-
-
-
-

Rising Stars: people with potential who you can help

-
-
-
-

24. UNCOVERING YOUR STRENGTHS

If you know me at all, you know I'm a HUGE strengths geek! I told you about how strengths are like super powers in Challenge #15. In this challenge, I'm giving you a fast, free way to uncover some of your strengths by answering a few questions.

> **Your Challenge**: Write down the first thing that comes to mind when you read each question. If it's taking too long, just skip it.

EXHILARATED:

What kind of activities make you feel alive?

COMPLIMENTS:

What kind of activities do other people say you are good at?

CRAVINGS:

What kind of activities do you naturally gravitate to?

LEARNING SPONGE:

What kind of information or activities do you easily grasp?

LOST IN THE ZONE:

What kinds of activities do you 'lose track of time' while doing?

GRATIFICATION:

What kinds of activities do you enjoy so much that you would do them for free?

STAND OUT:

What unique skills, strengths, and/or perspective do you bring to a group?

25. STARTING THE STRENGTHS CONVO

Understanding and applying strengths will increase your engagement, performance, productivity, teamwork, customer loyalty, retention, and financial gain.

> **Your Challenge**: Complete this challenge with someone who knows you well, such as a supervisor, colleague, mentor, family member. Use it as a way to understand and maximize the strengths of each person you work with. Question 4b should be answered with your partner, but everything else, you can complete and then share.

1. What do you like most about your job?

2. What 2-3 business activities do you do best, better than most people?

a. What do they feel like and result in?

3. What tasks and/or activities do you loathe in your job?

4. What is one goal you are currently focused on?

a. Which of your top strengths could you use to help achieve this goal?

b. Which of my top strengths could I use to help you achieve this goal?

5. What can someone who works with you, or cares about you, do to be a better partner to you?

6. How do you like to be recognized? Encouraged?

26. IDENTIFYING & BUILDING UPON STRENGTHS

To truly get the full benefits of your super powers, or your strengths, you have to constantly develop them. This challenge is designed to help you keep the momentum moving from the previous strengths challenges so cultivating and using your strengths can transform into daily habits!

Ask yourself these questions, or adapt them to ask a team member or someone you supervise. Do this on a weekly basis, ideally on Friday or at the end of the week.

WEEKLY QUESTIONS:

1. Which specific tasks/activities did you find yourself looking forward to last week?

2. Was there a time last week when you got into a "zone", finding it easy to concentrate and intrigued by the activity? If yes, describe how you felt, what were you doing, and the end result.

3. Was there a time last week when after completing an activity/ task, you felt powerful, knowledgeable, confident, or outstanding? If yes, describe how you felt, what you were doing, and the end result.

Your Challenge : Use these questions for 3-4 weeks, recording your answers below.

WEEK 1 Reflection:

_____

_____

_____

_____

_____

_____

WEEK 2 Reflection:

_____

_____

_____

_____

_____

_____

WEEK 3 Reflection:

_____

_____

_____

_____

_____

_____

WEEK 4 Reflection:

_____

_____

_____

_____

_____

_____

27. THE *ONE THING* PHILOSOPHY

The 'ONE Thing' philosophy changed my life and how I operate. My success and productivity have both dramatically increased by applying this philosophy (in both business and personal areas of my life), and it's based on the book, *The ONE Thing*, by Gary Keller and Jay Papasan.

The philosophy boils down to one simple thing the authors call the 'focusing question'. It states that in every situation, especially at the beginning of each day, or when tackling your to-do list, you should ask yourself the focusing question.

From personal experience I can tell you that asking this question combined with following through on your answer is a ***CATALYST MOVE!*** So much so that I have an app set to remind me of the question every hour. Additionally, it's posted on my wall in my office, right next to my monitor. You can find the app I use for the slick little reminders on the Catalyst Guide resource page at **discoveractengage.com**

The 'focusing question' comes down to identifying the lead domino and hitting it (working on it) until it falls, catalyzing the other dominos' movement to create amazing momentum.

If you're thinking, "Enough already! What's the *'focusing question'*?" Take a breath. You actually already know it, because we used it in Challenge #21…

"What's the ONE THING you can do such that by doing it everything else will be easier or unnecessary?"

SO I ask you…What's the ONE THING you can do such that by doing it everything else will be easier or unnecessary, RIGHT NOW?

Your Challenge: Identify your ONE THING for right now:

_____

(this could be related to a ***Someday Goal*** or a mini goal)

Reflect on how you came to this decision here:

_____

_____

_____

_____

_____

_____

_____

_____

28. POWER OF SMALL STEPS

Let's start by saying I have failed hundreds of times. In today's culture, we are encouraged to hide our failures and only promote and share about our successes. Please know... NO ONE has success, at least big, consistent success, without SOME FAILURES along the way. We often read about the 'overnight success' of Instagram or [insert any celebrity/expert name], but what we don't realize is that 'overnight' was 5, 10, 15, 40 years in the making. Don't believe me??? Google "overnight success" or "overnight success took years", read the results, and then tweet at me (@megwatt) that I was right. ☺

Now, back to the power of small steps. Success is built sequentially, one step at a time. Gretchen Rubin said it best — "What you do every day matters more than what you do once in a while." I've found this to be true whether I'm trying to accomplish a goal or build a new habit.

Here's a personal example of how I built a habit, including the failures and small steps I took daily in order to get there.

When I started my own business, I went on a kick of studying successful business owners, trying hard to learn about the habits they use regularly to obtain their success. I was SHOCKED by the number of people who mentioned a meditation practice. I always thought meditating was a little too WooWoo for me. But after 20+ successful people (yes it took me that many people to get over the WooWoo mindset and give it a try), I downloaded two free apps I'd heard mentioned several times — *Headspace* and *Calm.*

I tried it. I started with two or five minute guided meditations, and shot for doing it Monday through Friday. In the beginning, I failed miserably. I only did it once or twice a week and would sometimes go a several weeks without doing any sessions at all. Finally, I started setting small goals such as committing to two or three days a week, and then slowly increased the length of each session.

Over time, I built up my meditation length to 10-20 minutes and started doing it on a regular basis. As I write this book, 15 months have passed since I first 'started' my meditation practice, and I just celebrated a STREAK of 60 days in a row that I've meditated. That's right, what was at first a long, up and down battle, has transformed into me hitting 60 straight days of meditating. The best part? I'm loving it!

More on the benefits of meditating in Challenge #30...

You can see the proof of my 60-day streak on the Catalyst Guide resource page **discoveractengage.com,** and hopefully by the time you find yourself reading this, I'll have hit a new personal record.

The point of sharing my meditation practice journey with you is to emphasize the **power and importance of small steps**, because...

Consistent small steps lead to big results.

Your challenge: Think of ONE (yes only one. I mean it!) medium to large goal you want to accomplish, or a new habit you want to start. Then pick ONE (yes, again only one) small step you can start doing that will eventually lead to accomplishing your goal or building your new habit.

Your Goal or Habit:

_____

_____

_____

_____

Your ONE small step and your commitment to doing it:

_____

_____

_____

_____

Name one small thing you can do to help yourself be successful (hint: this could be like setting out your workout clothes the night before if you're trying to workout in the morning):

_____

_____

_____

_____

Ask yourself, why do you want to accomplish this goal or develop this habit?

_____

_____

_____

_____

_____

_____

_____

_____

_____

_____

_____

_____

_____

_____

29. TRACKING HABITS

Hopefully you've completed or at least read Challenge #28 about small steps, because we are going to build upon that in this Challenge. One of the ways I've been really successful in accomplishing goals, developing new habits, and enhancing existing habits, is to track my efforts. It sounds simple, and it is!

I created a habit tracking sheet when I was reading the book, *The Power of Habit: Why We Do What We Do in Life and Business* by Charles Duhigg, and it turns out that tracking my daily progress has been the key to my success. Once you get enough x's in a row, you'll stop wanting to break the chain of x's and have a blank spot; if you're like me, you get competitive with yourself. You'll see what I'm talking about soon.

Here's an example of a Habit Progress Tracker:

DAILY TASKS

TASK	SUN	MON	TUES	WED	THUR	FRI	SAT	SUN	MON	TUES	WED	THUR	FRI	SAT	SUN	MON	TUES	WED

TASK	SUN	MON	TUES	WED	THUR	FRI	SAT	SUN	MON	TUES	WED	THUR	FRI	SAT	SUN	MON	TUES	WED

Your challenge: Start tracking your progress! Creating habits can include anything from flossing regularly, to getting your inbox down to zero, to eating vegetables daily, to making 5 sales calls every day. What the tasks are don't matter. Start with small steps (e.g. eating at least one vegetable a day), and TRACK your progress DAILY!

You can create your own tracking sheet, download mine, or find an app to use. Download my habit tracking sheet from the Catalyst Guide resource page: **discoveractengage.com**

Here's an example of my Complete Habit Progress Tracker:

DAILY TASKS

TASK	SUN	MON	TUES	WED	THUR	FRI	SAT	SUN	MON	TUES	WED	THUR	FRI	SAT	SUN	MON	TUES	WED

TASK	SUN	MON	TUES	WED	THUR	FRI	SAT	SUN	MON	TUES	WED	THUR	FRI	SAT	SUN	MON	TUES	WED

WEEKLY TASKS

TASK	Week 1	Week 2	Week 3	Week 4	Wee

MONTHLY TASKS

TASK	Month:	Month:

30. MINDFULNESS & MEDITATION

Mindfulness and meditation are incredibly powerful and important tools in helping you accomplish your **Someday Goal**. You can read about my initial feeling on these topics in Challenge #28.

Meditation and mindfulness offer a ton of benefits, including improved memory, productivity, and stress relief. I'm not a researcher so I'm not going to share a ton of stats or facts about the benefits, but you can do your own Google search to read all about it (ideally from credible sources)!

I've personally experienced all the benefits I mentioned above from developing a personal meditation practice. You won't receive all of them in the beginning, but stick with it long enough, and you will.

Within the first 2 weeks I noticed that I was becoming more mindful of day to day irritants, like picking the "wrong" line at the grocery checkout and losing an extra five minutes. In those moments of irritation, I was suddenly able to calm myself down right away, mostly because I was aware of my feelings as opposed to just reacting to my gut like I had done in the past.

My favorite go-to mediation resource is the *Calm* app, and it's free! Beginners can learn the basics of mindfulness meditation with the app's *7 Days of Calm* program. This program was a **CATALYST MOVE** for me. I learned what mindfulness is about and it helped me start my meditation practice.

> **Your Challenge**: Give meditation a try. Whether on your own or with the *Calm* or *Headspace* app.

31. GRATITUDE

Gratitude is like coffee or sleep – you need it every day and it makes life better. I grew up with basic needs that were always met, but there were plenty of times where we didn't get any of the 'extra' or 'fun stuff' we wanted. Because of this, I always try to appreciate what I have, especially because I've been able to add to my lists of wants over the years. But real gratitude and cultivating a gratitude practice is an entirely separate thing, at an entirely different level.

I first learned about the importance of practicing gratitude when I launched into the world of entrepreneurship and found myself studying successful entrepreneurs. Much like meditation, almost everyone talked about gratitude as something they express often, even daily.

Here's what I've learned from keeping a gratitude journal over the last three years. In the beginning, writing in it was very hit or miss, with months skipping by between entries. But for the last year, I've written in one almost daily, and it's been a blast.

Yes, **practicing gratitude has been a BLAST!** It's made me a more positive person overall, and I can't begin to tell you how much I've enjoyed looking back at old entries. Best of all, this practice takes less than 5 minutes a day.

> **Your Challenge:** Start a gratitude journal! Try once a week at first, and eventually work your way up to daily.

CATALYST MOVES: I started simply listing 3 things I was grateful for every day before bedtime. Categories of gratitude I think about: people, opportunities, and simple things.

Recently, I started using *The Five Minute Journal.* You can find this on the Catalyst Guide resource page: **discoveractengage.com**

32. HEALTHY HABITS

Full disclosure – this is a topic and an area of my life that I struggled with for a VERY long time. Even when I knew what I should be doing, I ignored advice and thought I could muscle my way through. Now that I'm a little older, I've truly come to understand the importance and necessity of good self-care.

Whether you are a college student, entrepreneur, parent, or just a high achiever, I know you can relate to the feeling of sacrificing sleep, a well-balanced meal, or exercise to just get a 'few' more things done. There was a time when I was constantly making those sacrifices to get 'more' done – usually sacrificing in all 3 areas – and I had never been more sick in my life. I was riding the roller coaster of 100mph and then crashing and burning.

Watt's Lightbulb Moment: Once I hit my late twenties, I started realizing that the roller coaster wasn't sustainable and I needed better balance. Thanks to an amazing person who taught me the importance of good sleep and self-care, I'm way healthier now, and actually getting more done.

A few tips I've added to my life:
- Eating a green smoothie every morning
- Doing yoga!

CATALYST MOVE:
- Go to bed earlier, and commit to 7-8 hours of sleep on a regular basis. These small changes have had the biggest impact on my productivity and health.

   Your Challenge: Pick one area in your life that needs better healthy habits (eating, exercise, sleep, etc.) and do one small thing to start improving this area. Bonus points if you use Challenge #29 – Tracking Habits – to help you!

33. MY MANTRA

Companies define 'mantras' as an encapsulation of their brand position and make all decisions with it in mind. I define 'mantra' as a phrase or sentence that I refer to when making decisions also. Mantras help guide me, and remind me what's really important. A few of my past mantras include:

- Fill your cup (do things that add joy)
- If it's not a 'hell yes', it's a no (more on this one in #37)
- Do the right thing, not the easy thing
- Count it all joy
- "Your level of success will seldom exceed your level of personal development." - Jim Rohn

While the above have provided me a TON of value, there's one that has truly been a **CATALYST MOVE** for me and one that I hold on to year after year:

'Do the RIGHT thing, NOT the EASY thing.'

Whenever I want to skip meditation, hit the snooze, skimp on veggies, or cut other important or healthy tasks, I think to myself, "Do the right thing, not the easy thing". Most of the time, it's just the little nudge I need to stop being lazy and start doing the thing I *think* I want to skip.

> **Your Challenge:** Pick a mantra, whether it's one of the above, or one of your own, and try to use it this week.

Watt's Lightbulb Moment: When I first tried adopting a mantra, I had to put it EVERYWHERE to help it stay top of mind. This includes post-it notes on mirrors, screen savers, and phone wallpaper. I recommend plastering yours everywhere!

34. SAYING "NO" IS GOOD!

If you're like me, saying "no" often feels like a bad 4-letter word. As I try to say no, I hear a nagging voice in the back of my head say, "If you say *it*, you'll really be letting them down," or, "You won't be asked to do X again if *it* comes out." Does this happen to you too?

Whether you're a people pleaser, someone who thinks they can do it all, or just have a straight-up "no" phobia (I used to be a little of each), I want to tell you that **saying "no" is a good thing!**

CATALYST MOVE: Understanding and repeating the phrase, "If it's not a HELL YES, it's a NO!"

"Hell yes, or a NO." Those four words will change the trajectory of your life and work.

On the Catalyst Guide resource page, I've added some great articles about how to say "no" gracefully. Find them at **discoveractengage.com**.

> **Your Challenge**: Try saying "no" at least 3 times this week. Below, write down what you said "no" to and how saying it made you feel. Also, include the kinds of re-actions you got from the people you said "no" to, and whether they were good or bad.

_____

_____

_____

_____

35. BOOK RECOMMENDATIONS

First, I would like to give a shout-out to my family and childhood teachers: Me, Megan Watt, is giving book recommendations. I was NEVER a reader, and it wasn't until I finished 27 years of school (preschool to grad school), that I began truly enjoying reading and was able to start making it a habit. Now that I do enjoy reading, I want to share some of my favorite books.

Here they are – tweet-sized (or slightly longer) book descriptions including my #1 takeaway, which I'm calling **Watt's Lightbulb Moments.**

The Miracle Morning by **Hal Elrod:**

> ***Tweet***: 6 easy steps to do every morning that will CHANGE your life and help you to have the success you are destined for!

> ***Watt's Lightbulb Moment***: Why snoozing is bad and what message it sends to the world. I can get super pumped every morning about my day and my life by using the S.A.V.E.R.S.

Daring Greatly by **Brené Brown:**

> ***Tweet Description***: Learn how to develop the courage to show up and be seen. Without courage and vulnerability, we can't get creative, innovate, or learn.

> ***Watt's Lightbulb Moment***: Being an entrepreneur is vulnerable. It's all about cultivating the ability to handle and manage uncertainty. I discovered an amazing question: "What is worth doing, even if I fail?"

Start Something That Matters by **Blake Mycoskie:**

Tweet Description: An AMAZING journey of how Tom's Shoes got started and the importance of social entrepreneurship/just doing good in the world.

Watt's Lightbulb Moment: It's not bad to have a for-profit business that does good. More importantly, when you combine passion and ideas, the result is big. In the beginning you don't need to have all the answers – just get started!

Lean In by **Sheryl Sandberg**

Tweet Description: Women AND Men need to stand up and lean into women's rights to be at the table. Oh yeah, and there's a special place in hell for woman who don't help other women.

Watt's Lightbulb Moment: It's not about winning or losing, it's about showing up and being seen. Risk taking is important even though it's difficult. You'll never know what you're capable of if you don't try.

The ONE Thing by **Gary Keller and Jay Papasan**

Tweet Description: The BEST productivity book of ALL TIME. Multitasking is a lie. Real results come from focusing on ONE thing at a time.

Watt's Lightbulb Moment: Do the MOST important thing first, every day, and reserving 4 hours a day for it, no matter what it is. This book is a **CATALYST MOVE** for life & work.

36. BATCHING TASKS

The first time I heard about the concept of batching tasks was in the *4-Hour Work Week* by Tim Ferriss. What is batching? It's collecting a group of similar activities and doing them all at the same time. Some things you can batch include emails, cooking, meetings, phone calls, reading, interviewing, blogging, and time on social media, etc. If you were going to batch emails, you would limit yourself to checking it 1-3 times a day MAX. If you were to batch cooking, you'd make all of your meals, or at least complete the prep work, each Sunday, for the whole work week. Ultimately, batching saves time and stress!

Your Challenge: Try batching for 1 week, 1 task at a time!

This week **I am going to batch**: _____

Watt's Lightbulb Moment: Personally, I saved the most time when I started batching my meetings (Tuesdays & Thursdays), and limiting myself to only checking email twice a day – Around 11am or 1pm, and again at 4 or 5pm.

Turning off all push notifications on my phone and computer, and the little red badge notification icon on my phone were ***CATALYST MOVES!*** I was instantly free of the unbearable distraction of glancing at my phone to find the inbox number had jumped three times higher!

Pro tip! Try turning your phone to do not disturb (DND) every time you sit down to blast through tasks. I also always set an alarm to remember to turn DND off, but while it's on, it's incredibly helpful.

37. NO MORE MULTITASKING

Multitasking is a myth. Jumping from one thing to another is exhausting and ineffective. Every time we become distracted, it takes an average of 15 minutes to regain complete focus. These facts aren't just my opinion – there's plenty of research to back this up, most of which you can read in *The One Thing*.

I remember when my days were filled with interruptions. Every five minutes, my phone made some ding or buzz. That's no way to live and, thankfully, not how I operate anymore…most days. Life still happens sometimes.

Watt's Lightbulb Moment: When I committed to focusing on ONE task at a time, my productivity and success skyrocketed.

Your Challenge: Try committing to working on only ONE task at a time, in one hour increments!

For the next hour **I am going to focus on this ONE task**:

_____

For the next hour **I am going to focus on this ONE task**:

_____

For the next hour **I am going to focus on this ONE task**:

_____

CATALYST MOVE: Using the 'Pomodoro' Technique.

There's a great tool to help you with implementing the Pomorodo Technique. I use it every day, and it's free. Jump over to the Catalyst Guide resource page and check it out **discoveractengage.com**.

38. GTD –THE MOST IMPORTANT 3 LETTERS TO YOUR PRODUCTIVITY

GTD is a three letter word as common in my world as LOL, and I can tell you that when I GTD, I get to LOL at everyone else who didn't GTD that day.

GTD is short for **Getting Things Done**, a book and productivity art form by David Allen.

A few of my favorite key GTD principles:

1. Have an inbox for everything. This includes creating an inbox for tangible things like mail/paper stuff, and using your default email inbox.

2. Your inbox (physical or digital) is NOT a to do list, its purpose is to temporarily collect new items until you have time to sort them.

3. When sorting your inbox, for every item ask:

    a. What is it?

    b. Is it actionable?

4. The power of three simple words: *Do, Delegate, Defer.*

Watt's Lightbulb Moment: After attending a 2-3 day GTD training, I felt like I had to implement everything, but my complete overhaul wasn't sustainable. It's like developing any new habit – you need to build up to what you're trying to achieve. Soon, I realized I could adapt some of the GTD principles into things that were already working for me.

Your Challenge: Try doing one of the GTD principles or create your own system that helps you get more done!

CATALYST MOVE: Create a packing list, so you never forget anything again. Get my Evernote packing list on the Catalyst Guide resource page: **discoveractengage.com**.

_____   _____

_____   _____

_____   _____

_____   _____

_____   _____

_____   _____

_____   _____

_____   _____

_____   _____

_____   _____

_____   _____

_____   _____

39. TIME SAVING HACKS/TOOLS

In Challenges #36-38, we tackled different ideas and strategies to help you become more efficient. This is the **Act.** section of the Catalyst Guide, so it only makes sense that it would help you take more action. Now, I want to share some of my favorite time saving hacks and tools (in no particular order).

- **Facebook Newsfeed Eradicator** – It does what is sounds like it does – completely deletes your news feed. This allows you to log on and check on a friend or send a message without being distracted by some random person's life update.

- **Remove ALL notifications** – This includes sounds, lock screen, badges, etc. from all of the apps on your phone except for calls and texts.

- **Stop PUSHing information** – Stop your email (or other time burglar apps) from automatically pushing new items to your phone. Instead, you only get the new stuff when you decide to go into the app

CATALYST MOVE: **Start using Unroll.me**. It's a magical email tool that will unsubscribe you from any unwanted email lists. For the ones you want to keep, just roll them up into one daily email or decide to keep them in your inbox.

> **Your Challenge**: Try doing only ONE of these time saving hacks, or implement one tool.

Watt's Lightbulb Moment: Once I started using time saving hacks, my productivity skyrocketed. Whatever you do, don't Google "best time saving hacks" – I swear you'll lose 15-120 minutes. I've already done that for you. Try one of the above, and once you've started saving time, try another. You can spend time investigating more tools once you've given yourself more time by utilizing these.

40. PRODUCTIVITY TIPS/TOOLS

This is the last Challenge in the **Act.** section of the Catalyst Guide, and I wanted to go out with a bang to help you become EVEN MORE productive, because increased productivity means you are one step closer to achieve your ***Someday Goal!!***

Some resources I love, in no particular order:

- **Toggl** (app, web) – time tracking tool
- **Boomerang** (browser extension) – email tool
- **LastPass** (app, web) – never forget a password again
- **Asana** (app, web) – project management tool
- **IF** (app; aka "If this, then that") – and fun & useful
- **Inbox Pause** (browser extension) – email tool
- **Hootsuite** (app, desktop, web) – social media manager
- **Unroll.me** (app, web) – email declutter tool
- **Stay Focusd** (browser extentsion) – time burglar protection

CATALYST MOVES:
- **Sign up for Evernote** (app, desktop, web) – remember everything
- **Sign up for Dropbox** (app, desktop, web) – access everything

These are hands-down, of all the tools I've ever tried or researched, the top tools of all time. I use them to organize all facets of my personal and work life.

> **Your Challenge**: Try doing only ONE of these time saving hacks, or implement one tool.

Watt's Lightbulb Moment: Remembering the KISS method (keep it simple silly). Productivity is an entire industry, and it's easy to think we will be more productive once we get the right app for this or system for that. At the end of the day, doing what's most simple for you and discovering a system that works is what's going to change your life. One of my favorite tools is a paper-and-pen daily checklist system I created. Find it for download at **discoveractengage.com**.

Engage.

Identify who can help you achieve your *Someday Goal!*

"You are 76.7% more likely to achieve a goal when you share it with others!"

— The ONE Thing

*Based on a study by Dr. Gail Matthews

41. SHARE YOUR PAIL LIST

In Challenge #6, you created a Pail List. Hopefully you've learned that by writing a goal down, you're almost 40% more likely to achieve it. Mission accomplished in Challenge #6.

Now I want you to increase those odds to over 75% more likely to achieving your goal by doing one simple thing: just share it!!!

> **Your Challenge**: Write down each of your Pail List items and identify who you will share it with and whether or not you plan on doing a blanket announcement using social media platforms.

Pail List Item	**Who/How You'll Share It**

42. SHARE YOUR BUCKET LIST

This Challenge may look quite similar to the previous one, and you're right! But here, we're raising the stakes. In Challenge #5, you created a Bucket List, and now you know the correlation between writing a goal down and likeliness of achieving it. I've said it before, but it's worth mentioning again – you increase the odds of successfully achieving a goal to over *75% more likely* when you share it with someone else.

You guessed it. Now I want you to take a bigger step toward achieving your goals, and for many of you, this will be a vulnerable move. 35 Challenges ago you may have thought, "*What a fun exercise to imagine bucket list items.*" Fast forward, and now you're thinking, "*She wants me to do what????*"

Stay calm, I'm only asking you to take baby steps. Remember Challenge #28 – the Power of Small Steps!

> **Your Challenge**: Share some of your bucket list items with a few people, or all of it with one other person.

Bucket List/Item	Who You'll Share It With
_____	_____
_____	_____
_____	_____
_____	_____
_____	_____

43. SHARE YOUR ***SOMEDAY GOAL***

I bet you're noticing a pattern, and no, I'm not crazy. There's a reason to have you do basically the same thing over and over again. I'm intentionally raising the stakes, and hopefully, your confidence, before we really GO BIG!

That's right, I want you to share your ***Someday Goal*** with someone. Now, before you freak out or blast me on social media saying I've gone too far, I'm going to *dare greatly* (aka take a risk) by going first.

My ultimate ***Someday Goal*** is to build a life of fulfillment and joy. While this ***Someday Goal*** is the ultimate guide for my life, there's actually another one that truly serves as my compass when making decisions.

The ***Someday Goal*** I am currently tenaciously chasing is to speak to an audience of at least 10,000 people. It's a BIG goal and I'm in the early stages of climbing this mountain, but I'm making daily progress. Now it's your turn!

> **Your Challenge**: Think about your ***Someday Goal*** and who in your life has earned the right to hear it. List those people below and the date you plan on sharing it with them.

Who You'll Share It With   ## Due Date

_____   _____

_____   _____

_____   _____

P.S. I was bold and shared mine in front of everybody reading this book! I *know* you can share it with one person. ☺

44. THE POWER 100 LIST

The Power 100 List is something I learned from Adam Carroll, a friend and member of my Dream Team (he's one of my *Industry Insiders*). Adam describes this list as "a list of the 100 people in your life that like, love, and respect you." That may seem like a lot, but we've all got 100 people in our lives. They don't have to be BFFs or even people you see and talk to all the time. The only requirement is that they like, love, and respect you.

When I started Dream Catalyst Labs (DCL), I waited 7 months before sharing the news with my Power 100 List, which has since grown to 300.

The reasons behind waiting is another story for another time.

Some of the people on that list were grad school professors I hadn't talked to in years, but who I remembered having a great relationship with while we were on campus together.

Those professors were some of the first people to respond back to my DCL launch letter. I was forever grateful I thought to add them to my list instead of worrying about the amount of time that had gone by since we last spoke.

I share that story with you to encourage you to dig deep and build your list! 9 times out of 10, people don't count the years that have gone by; they're simply going to be happy to hear from you!

> **Your Challenge**: Think about all the people you've come to know from all of the different stages or seasons of your life, and identify your Power 100 List. Write their names down below.

1._____   18._____   35._____

2._____   19._____   36._____

3._____   20._____   37._____

4._____   21._____   38._____

5._____   22._____   39._____

6._____   23._____   40._____

7._____   24._____   41._____

8._____   25._____   42._____

9._____   26._____   43._____

10._____   27._____   44._____

11._____   28._____   45._____

12._____   29._____   46._____

13._____   30._____   47._____

14._____   31._____   48._____

15._____   32._____   49._____

16._____   33._____   50._____

17._____   34._____   51._____

52._____   69._____   87._____

53._____   71._____   88._____

54._____   72._____   89._____

55._____   73._____   90._____

56._____   74._____   91._____

57._____   75._____   92._____

58._____   76._____   93._____

59._____   77._____   94._____

60._____   78._____   95._____

61._____   79._____   96._____

62._____   80._____   97._____

63._____   81._____   98._____

64._____   82._____   99._____

65._____   83._____   100._____

66._____   84._____

67._____   85._____

68._____   86._____

45. SET REMINDERS TO CHECK-IN

The first several Challenges in the ***Engage.*** section have all been about sharing things with people and identifying important people in your life. We are going to dive into different strategies and ideas for how to nurture those relationships.

A great strategy for keeping in touch with people, especially the ones you don't see regularly, is to set a monthly or quarterly reminder on your calendar. If you use a project management or CRM tool, that works great too! This reminder is a cue to check in with them and make some kind of contact to get back on their radar. You can send an email, text, call, or even snail mail. Pick whatever you are most likely to do, and do that.

CATALYST MOVE: Send some snail mail. Everyone loves getting something in the mail, and now more than ever, it's rare and will definitely stand out.

> **Your Challenge**: Identify people you want to keep in touch with on a regular to semi-regular basis. Determine the frequency of communication you want with that person and what tool you'll use for a reminder.

_____

_____

_____

_____

_____

Watt's Lightbulb Moment: Creating a reminder is critical, because if you think you'll remember next month that you wanted to call Pat, you're wrong. Get it out of your head and written down, or you'll lose it! Bonus? When you spend less energy worrying, you have more brain space to get things done!

46. SEND ARTICLES OF VALUE

Another idea of how to nurture relationships – friends, potential clients, a Dream Team member, current/existing clients, or anybody else – is to maintain communication so you stay at the top of their mind on a regular to semi-regular basis. 'Semi-regular' can range anywhere from 1 month to 1 year to 5+ years. Obviously, it completely depends on who it is and the goals of that relationship. Point is, it's ON YOU to make the effort. Do not count on anybody else to take the first step.

Watt's Lightbulb Moment: Results, success, achieving goals, and reaching *Someday Goals* happen for those who take action and follow up. It's that simple...*and* that hard!

Another idea for nurturing relationships is to send articles, books, or other resources of value when trying to get back on their radar. The *of value* part is critical. If you know someone is starting a new job, and you come across (or even better take the time to do a little research) an article about 5 ways to successfully transition into a new role, could be a huge value to them. This strategy is extremely effective when seeking out potential mentors or new clients, but can be used in any type of relationship. The best part? It's easy to do.

> **Your Challenge**: Identify 5 people whose radar you want to get on this month, then pick the type of article/resource that would be a 'value add', and set a date for when you'll send it to them.

CATALYST MOVE: Create a task or reminder to do this!

47. SHARE WINS & LIFE EVENTS

Sticking with our theme, which is a critical part of the **Engage.** phase of achieving **Someday Goals**, I want to share another strategy I use to nurture relationships. This one seems almost too obvious, but we often take it for granted.

Tell people in your life, especially your Power 100 list when you have a win, new accomplishment, or a life event occurs.

Sometimes we think we do this with our social media posts. For the most part, social media announcements are very passive. It's only by chance that the people who we really hope to see our posts, do, and there's little to no intentionality behind it. How are they supposed to know it's for them?

My advice is to send specific communication to a specific set of people letting them know the new great thing that's happened in your life. As long as sharing your wins is not the only type of communication you have, most people won't think you're showing off. People love to hear about what's going well in their friends' lives, and honestly, you can't worry about how someone will interpret your success.

Additionally, if you're already surrounding yourself with success cheerleaders who are also working on achieving their goals, celebrating successes is one of the most rewarding things you can do together. Sharing your successes is like giving them a gift that says, "You can do it too!"

Watt's Lightbulb Moment: There will always be people who are jealous of, discount, or even judge your news, but from my experience, that's a much smaller number than the number of people who are truly excited for you and want to help celebrate with you. Please remember to have tact when sharing your news. Tact includes the tone your message has, the intent, and intentionality to stay humble. No matter what my news/success is, there are people in the world and probably on my list receiving my update who have done more exciting things than me. So, remember to have gratitude when sharing. And that is NOT an excuse for NOT sharing, or for watering down your win!

Your Challenge: Share a win or new life event with someone today!

48. OFFER TO HELP

When you flip the script on networking, or what I call 'connecting' (check out my "*Power of Connection*" activity), the game changes in your favor. What do I mean? Often, people go into a ~~networking~~ 'connecting' event thinking the point is to find a new client or mentor for an idea. Basically, they are trying *to get something*. My suggestion it to flip it from *getting* to *giving*. Going into any situation with the mindset of *giving* rather than *getting*, is a 100% **CATALYST MOVE.**

What happens when you have a *giving* mindset? You're more relaxed in the situation because there's less pressure on you to succeed. With a *get* mindset, the pressure is on to get what you came for, and if you don't get it, it feels like a loss. On the other hand, when you have a giving mindset, you're more likely to go in with an authentic approach. You'll be asking yourself questions like, "How can I help someone?" and the worst case scenario becomes that you didn't find somebody to help. It won't feel like a loss. It will just feel like the timing wasn't right.

So what does the giving mindset look like in practice? It's simple. Offer to help someone!! Yes, that's it. You can offer to help with a task, to make an introduction or connection, or to just listen. Really, all you have to do is make the offer and ask, "Is there anything I can help you with right now or in the future?"

Watt's Lightbulb Moment: This simple question changed my life: *Is there anything I can help you with right now or in the future?* Asking this question is a **CATALYST MOVE**. Most people are stunned by the question, some people will take you up on your offer, and some are just pleasantly surprised you took the time to ask.

> **Your Challenge**: Offer to help someone today by asking, "How can I help?" or another variation.

49. ENLISTING JOB SEARCH HELP

This is the last strategy for now about nurturing relationships. Some of you may wonder why I spent so many challenges on this topic. The answer is simple: it's ***that important*** of a topic.

Life is all about people. Whether it's work, fun, family, insert any area of life, *people* is at the core. I've always loved the saying *We do business with people we know, like, and trust.* I completely agree with that, and know that the only way to find the people who know, like, and trust us is to build relationships. A critical ingredient to building relationships is taking the time to nurture them. Remember, we all need a little water sometimes.

Watt's Lightbulb Moment: What you put into the universe comes back to you. If you put out exactly what you're looking for in a new job (or partner or opportunity), you'll be pleasantly surprised at how often you find that effort or thought boomeranged back to you. It's happened to me hundreds of times, including when I landed some dream jobs and took the leap to start my own business.

The next time you're job searching or looking for some other new opportunity, let your Power 100 list and/or your Dream Team (at the very least) know:

1) that you are searching and 2) what you're looking for!

Your Challenge: Think of something you're looking for in life. It could be a new job, client, hair stylist, whatever. Now, tell people that you're looking for it.

CATALYST MOVES: 1) Do this all the time, for anything. I recently did it when trying to find the best credit card and airline miles program. 2) Track your results. Do you experience the boomerang effect? FYI, this concept is also called the 'law of attraction'.

50. DEVELOP YOUR DREAM TEAM – CHEERLEADERS

You've learned what I believe to be 5 awesome and important strategies for nurturing relationships. Some of the most important people in your world are going to be on your Dream Team. Because of that, they are the most important people to spend time nurturing and developing relationships with. The following challenges are going to be straightforward and pretty familiar.

> **Your Challenge**: Use one of the five ideas from Challenges #45-49, and reach out to each Cheerleader on your Dream Team.

CATALYST MOVES:

1) Reach out to at least one, if not all of the people on your Dream Team Cheerleaders list this week!

2) Track how often you communicate with them, and be sure to have reminders in place so you're reaching out consistently.

You can list here which Cheerleader(s) you're going to reach out to, which strategy you're going to use, and when you're going to use it.

_____

_____

_____

_____

_____

51. DEVELOP YOUR DREAM TEAM – INDUSTRY INSIDERS

If you completed Challenge #50, you know the drill. Don't waste any time. Get started on building a stronger relationship with your Industry Insiders.

For a refresher on your Dream Team, or on the different roles, head back to Challenge #23 where you first identified your Dream Team members.

> **Your Challenge**: Use one of the five ideas from Challenges #45-49, and reach out to each Industry Insider on your Dream Team.

CATALYST MOVES:

1) Reach out to at least one, if not all of them this week!

2) Track how often you communicate with them, and be sure to have reminders in place so you're reaching out consistently.

You can list here which Industry Insider(s) you're going to reach out to, which strategy you're going to use, and when you're going to use it.

_____

_____

_____

_____

_____

52. DEVELOP YOUR DREAM TEAM – CONNECTORS

If you did Challenge #50 & #51, you know what to do. Don't waste any time, and get started on building a stronger relationship with your Connectors.

For a refresher on your Dream Team, or on the different roles, head back to Challenge #23 where you first identified who was on your Dream Team.

> **Your Challenge**: Use one of the five ideas from Challenges #45-49, and reach out to each Connector on your Dream Team.

CATALYST MOVES:

1) Reach out to at least one, if not all of them, this week!

2) Track how often you communicate with them, and be sure to have reminders in place so you're reaching out consistently.

You can list here which Connector(s) you're going to reach out to, which strategy you're going to use, and when you're going to use it.

_____

_____

_____

_____

_____

53. DEVELOP YOUR DREAM TEAM – MOMENTUM MOVERS

You're catching on. Now it's time to start building a stronger relationship with your Momentum Movers.

For a refresher on your Dream Team or on the different roles, head over to Challenge #23 where you first identified who was on your Dream Team.

> **Your Challenge**: Use one of the five ideas from Challenges #45-49, and reach out to each Momentum Mover on your Dream Team.

CATALYST MOVES:

1) Reach out to at least one, if not all, of them this week!

2) Track how often you communicate with them, and be sure to have reminders in place so you're reaching out consistently.

You can list here which Momentum Mover(s) you're going to reach out to, which strategy you're going to use, and when you're going to use it.

_____

_____

_____

_____

_____

54. DEVELOP YOUR DREAM TEAM – OUTLIERS

Don't let your Outliers be on the outside of your communication and relationship nurturing plan. Get started on building a stronger relationship with your Outliers today!

For a refresher on your Dream Team or on the different roles, head back to Challenge #23 where you first identified who was on your Dream Team.

> **Your Challenge**: Use one of the five ideas from Challenges #45-49, and reach out to each Outlier on your Dream Team.

CATALYST MOVES:

1) Reach out to at least one, if not all, of them this week!

2) Track how often you communicate with them, and be sure to have reminders in place so you're reaching out consistently.

You can list here which Outlier(s) you're going to reach out to, which strategy you're going to use, and when you're going to use it.

_____

_____

_____

_____

_____

55. DEVELOP YOUR DREAM TEAM – RISING STARS

Last, but certainly not least, reach out to your Rising Stars. Rising Stars are some of the most important people on your Dream Team because they are the next generation and their impact potential is huge. When you help develop your Rising Stars, they will eventually start turning into the stars you knew they could be, and you'll get to watch them become Industry Insiders or Connectors for other people. Eventually, they will have their own Rising Stars. The ripple effect is where we will start to see some EPIC impact and positive change!

Don't waste any more time – get started on building a stronger relationship with your Rising Stars.

> **Your Challenge**: Use one of the five ideas from Challenges #45-49, and reach out to each Rising Star on your Dream Team.

CATALYST MOVES:

1) Reach out to at least one, if not all, of them this week!

2) Track how often you communicate with them, and be sure to have reminders in place so you're reaching out consistently.

You can list here which Rising Star(s) you're going to reach out to, which strategy you're going to use, and when you're going to use it.

_____

_____

_____

56. CONNECTING ON LINKEDIN

Next, we are going to dive into some tips to improve the way we connect with others to unleash the real *Power of Connection*! Connecting tips, more commonly known as networking tips, can help you improve your game and your overall impact.

One of my favorite ways to connect is using LinkedIn (LI). It's robust, global, and great for both extroverts and introverts.

In no particular order, here are some of my favorite LinkedIn tips:

- Personalize your invitation to connect by reminding the person how you met and/or what you talked about. Include why you're connecting with them if you've never met.

- Send out invitations to connect shortly after meeting someone or attending an event.

- Build Your List of Potential Employers or clients

  o Do an advanced people search to find *decision makers*

- Set up informational interviews.

- Have an awesome summary:

  o It should include what you do, how you can help, who you help, and a call to action (CTA).

  o Remember, people skim a profile in 5 seconds so it pays to be clear, concise, and to use bullets and spacing appropriately.

- In order for your profile to be search engine-friendly, your last name needs to be visible and your profile needs to be public.

- o A LI profile is almost guaranteed to be within the top five results when your name is searched, and it's usually in the top 3. This is a great thing if you don't have your own website!

- Update your profile regularly to keep it current

- Create a 'vanity' URL… instead of the default URL, customize your profile with your name. For example, mine is LinkedIn.com/in/MeganWatt

- LI's 'advanced search' feature is SUPER powerful and gets very specific.

  - o This helps you get really clear about who your target is (company or person or group).

  - o Seeking to connect with a thought leader? Comment on their articles or find them on social media platforms so you can like/share their content.

  - o All GIVE, and no pitch.

- Once you find these people, get on their radar!

  - o Send a custom connection request, create rapport, and show what you have in common.

  - o When they say yes, and connect with you, you've built traction, so build on it!

- Learn more tips at blog.linkedin.com – anything by Lindsay Pollak is gold.

Your Challenge: Pick ONE of the tips above and do it today. If your profile is below par, start there first. Then, move into tips for engaging with people.

CATALYST MOVE: Get active on LinkedIn sooner rather than later, and implement as many of these strategies as possible.

Watt's Lightbulb Moment: LinkedIn is NOT only for job seekers, and people in sales or HR. It's for everyone, and YOU should be on it!

57. CONNECTING AT LIVE EVENTS

Face to face connections are incredibly valuable opportunities to build new relationships and nurture existing ones. The problem is, so many people go about it all wrong.

Below are some of my favorite tips and strategies to effectively connect at live events!

- **Practice asking open ended questions** to spark personalized connections rather than just small talk.

  o Instead of easy to answer questions (e.g. where do you work) or surface level topics (e.g. how about the weather lately), ask specific questions.

  o Ask questions that spur conversation among groups.

- **Ask better questions** – go to Challenge #58 for a ton of great questions that are ALL better than, "What do you do?"

- **Take advantage of the expertise in the room**

  o Ask other attendees why they attended the event or joined the organization. What benefits have they received and what have they learned from participating?

- **Get to the networking event early because…**

  o It's less intimidating.

  o That's why you're there.

- **Wear something that stands out** *(I love wearing my red pants)*

  o Fun clothes can provide great conversation starters.

  o And if you have to leave early, more people will remember seeing you because they will remember your bright attire.

- **Go into the event with 3-5 questions prepared** – then you won't have to spend as much time thinking of your feet.

CATALYST MOVE: Be interested, not interesting!

  o Rather than keeping the focus on you, ask others about their projects and goals.

  o Attentively listen and ask further questions. Suggest resources or connections that may be helpful to their endeavors.

Watt's Lightbulb Moment: NONE of these tips matter if you don't follow up! I'm not joking. Following up and utilizing the *Power of Connection* is one of the #1 keys to success. It's so important that I've dedicated an entire Challenge to it. Jump to Challenge #59 for follow-up strategies.

Your Challenge: Pick ONE of the tips above and use it at the next opportunity.

Pro Tip: If you consider yourself an introvert or somebody who's just bad at small talk, I highly recommended *The Fine Art of Small Talk* by Debra Fine. I've hired her before to speak at events about small talk, and there are hundreds of great tips in there. You can find more information about this book and other resources to ***Engage.*** at the Catalyst Guide resource page: **discoveractengage.com**.

58. GOOD QUESTIONS TO ASK

I believe many people hate (or strongly dislike ~~networking~~ connecting events because they dread answering the default question, "What do you do?" dozens of times. Have you ever considered what it would be like to answer that question if you dislike what you do or if you were in between jobs? My guess is that many of you have fallen into one or both of those categories before.

You have the POWER to CHANGE this by doing one super simple and easy thing… ASK BETTER QUESTIONS!

Some great questions to start with:

- What are some of your goals this year and how are you working toward them? *(chance to learn about projects, passions, or something else)*

- If you could travel anywhere in the world, where would you go and why? *(chance to make a connection)*

- Where are you from? *(chance to make a connection, "I know someone from there too")*

- What are you excited about in the next few weeks or months? *(can highlight what gives the person energy)*

- What do you like to do in your free time outside of work? *(can uncover shared interests or beneficial opportunities)*

- What are your favorite restaurants in the area? *(can give ideas of new restaurants to try in your own community or good places to check out if in an unknown area)*

- Why did you decide to attend this event, and what have been your key takeaways? *(can spur discussion about the event, speaker, etc.)*

- What is a **Someday Goal** you have? *(can be the spawn of powerful connection!)*

  Your Challenge: Pick ONE of these above questions and use it at the next opportunity.

59. FOLLOW UP STRATEGIES

I've mentioned on SEVERAL occasions the importance of building and nurturing relationships with people. One of the MOST important parts of all of the above is what you do to follow up. So that you never miss the opportunity to follow up again, here are 30 strategies for making it happen!!

1) Tell them about a book, article, video, or website that might help with what you talked about.

2) Send a personal note. If it's a prospective client, include a copy of your marketing material.

3) Tell them about an upcoming event that addresses an issue you think they have.

4) Invite them to an event where you are a speaker, organizer, or sponsor.

5) Attend an event where you are likely to run into them.

6) Send a nice-to-meet-you or good-to-see-you note with your business card.

7) Call or email to ask what's new in their world.

8) Ask them to meet you for coffee, a drink, or lunch.

9) Invite them for golf, tennis, a bike ride, or a walk in the park, concert, play, reading, or art opening.

10) Offer to stop by their place of business.

11) If following up with a prospective client, send a letter summarizing what you last talked about and suggesting next steps.

12) Send them an article (or link to one) that you have written.

13) Send them an article someone else has written about a topic relevant to them.

14) Send them a present – chocolate, cookies, flowers, a plant, a bottle of wine, or a book.

15) Send them a birthday card.

16) Send them a joke or cartoon about their industry or your field.

17) Send a postcard reminding them what you do.

18) Offer them a free sample of what you can do for them.

19) Send an announcement about a new development in your business.

20) Send a copy of your newsletter or post from your blog and invite them to subscribe.

21) Send a link to a print, audio, or video interview you're in that highlights your work.

22) Refer a business prospect.

23) Watch for their posts on Facebook, Twitter, or LinkedIn and comment on them.

24) Post something useful to an online community where they are members.

25) Post a comment on their blog.

26) Invite them to visit your updated website.

27) Invite them to an open house, webinar, reception, demonstration, or free workshop.

28) Host a networking breakfast or brown bag lunch and invite several people and prospects.

29) Offer to give a talk or brown bag lunch for their organization at no charge.

30) Write a white paper or case study and send it to all your prospects.

CATALYST MOVE: Be a Connector!! Introduce them to a connection of yours they might like to know.

Watt's Lightbulb Moment: Always remember to focus on what you can do for others. What you give always comes back to you! It's the ancient principle of sowing and reaping.

> **Your Challenge**: Pick three of these strategies above and use it at the next opportunity. Ideally, use ONE right now!!

60. FINDING PEOPLE TO CONNECT WITH

So far in the **Engage.** section of this Catalyst Guide, I've given you 15 Challenges on building and nurturing relationships, packed full of strategies and tips. There should be ZERO excuse for not staying connected to people.

If you're wondering how to find the people to use all of these awesome strategies on, you're in luck. Did you really think I'd take you this far down the *Power of Connection* tunnel and not show you where to find people in the first place?

"Here are some great places to start finding people to add to your Dream Team (Challenge #23), to your Power 100 List (Challenge #44), or to just do some informational interviews with. Maybe you'll even find a new friend or mentor in the process.

Where to Find People to Engage & Increase Your Network:

- Associations
- Business Networking Groups/events
- Alumni Networking Groups/events
- Service Clubs
- Religious institutions
- Community events
- LinkedIn Groups
- Twitter Chats
- Facebook Groups
- Coffee shops
- Airplanes

- Classes
- Retreats
- Workshops
- Conferences
- Meetups
- Gym
- Blogging
- Dog park

Your Challenge: Pick ONE of these places and START meeting people. Pick the MOST appealing one so you'll actually do it, and have fun!

THE CONCLUSION

You did it!! You've either completed all of the challenges, or you've just made it this far into the book. Either way, it's a big deal, but I hope it's because of the first reason, and you were able to begin conquering fears and accomplishing goals!

First, thank you for taking the opportunity to invest in yourself, and for allowing me to play a part in that (there's more appreciation and gratitude for you in the "Practicing Gratitude - acknowledgements" section, so don't miss that). Second, give yourself a HUGE high five and/or hug, and take a virtual air high five from me!! If you even did one challenge in this book, you've made progress toward reaching your *Someday Goals*. I do mean "did" too, and not just "read". Learning is important, and I'm so glad you read this book, BUT if you don't take one single action step, I haven't done my job. Truthfully, you really do learn best by doing, and that's why the goal of this ~~book~~ Catalyst Guide is to inspire and motivate you to take real action toward your *Someday Goals*.

For many of you, I know you took massive action while reading this Catalyst Guide, and are already making huge steps forward. Congrats to you, but please don't stop! Another HUGE key to success and to accomplishing *Someday Goals* is to ride the momentum and keep building upon it. Your journey will have lots of twists and turns along the way, but you HAVE to KEEP GOING. When you stumble or fail (it's not if, it's when), throw grace in your face, and just keep going.

"Throwing grace in your face" is an expression I use when I need a reminder to be kind to myself, to focus on the positives, and to remember what I have accomplished, as opposed to laughing and pointing at myself. Even worse is to give up when there's mud on your face from stumbling. We all stumble. We all have setbacks. Therefore, we've all had mud on our faces at some point or another, and can look forward to more mud in the future! When this happens to ourselves or to others, remember to be kind, throw grace, and offer understanding as opposed to offering shame, guilt, or fear.

Lastly, remember that many of these 60 Challenges can be done multiple times. Feel free to revisit and add more! Maybe you want to add something new to your bucket list or a new member to your Dream Team. If you have not gone to **discoveractengage.com** yet, be sure to check out the Catalyst Guide bonuses and additional resources!

A SPECIAL INVITATION

FREE Bonus Gift for YOU!

To help you achieve your **Someday Goals** I've included a TON of FREE Resources for you at:

DiscoverActEngage.com

Resources include templates, examples, and all of the tools I mention in the book – I utilize all these in my own life and business to help me accomplish my **Someday Goals**.

Visit **DiscoverActEngage.com** to stay connected with the *Discover. Act. Engage.* community and connect with like-minded individuals who are already taking action toward their **Someday Goals.** Together, we will design the future of the community!

If you would like to connect with me personally on social media, follow me on Twitter @megwatt or connect with me on LinkedIn at Linkedin.com/in/meganwatt

MY DREAM JOB JOURNEY

For all of the people who hired me into unexpected Dream Jobs, and for all the people I worked with, THANK YOU! I wanted to share with all of the Dream Jobs I've had over the years, and what I took away from each experience (jobs are listed chronologically).

Rotunda Movie Store, *Clerk*, age 15

I never thought I'd be able to trade in my nursing home job for a job that would allow me to watch movies, eat pizza, make money, and talk all day. It was exactly what I needed at this time in my life.

Palm Island Resort – Kids Club, *Counselor*, age 16

At this job, I was paid to be outside playing with kids. I planned adventures, drove a golf cart, hung out with a real pirate – Red Beard – and got the best tan of my life. Opportunities like this really helped shape me into the positive, community-oriented person I am today.

Palm Island Resort – General Store, *Store Clerk*, age 17

I continued working on the island, made a little more money, got free food and ice cream, and played games in the restaurant when we were empty because of bad weather. I even got a barge pass that I *might* have continued using long after my employment had ended. Call it good on this? Again, working for this company provided me an incredibly fun and lighthearted experience.

Megan Watt

Florida State University – The Ogelsby Union, *Student Employee*, age 20

You gave me a job because I had WAY too much time on my hands after Dance Marathon ended. By the end of my 2+ years there, you had hired at least four of my good friends, and you even allowed me to be on a search committee and represent the student voice when the "Student Activities Center Dream Team" decided to completely vacate their roles within a 4 month period, leaving me stranded for my victory lap (aka my 5th year). The remaining staff and the new staff were amazingly supportive and continued to let me be involved in some amazing projects and opportunities. You 'allowed' me to do a ton of work for DM during our busy times (well, maybe, "You didn't fire me for doing it," is more accurate). It's here where I met one of the most talented and supportive women I've ever known, a woman who ended up being like a second mother to me while mine was 5.5 hours away, and even made her husband hire me when I needed a job between college and grad school.

Indiana University – Career Development Center, *Graduate Assistant*, age 23

When you hired me, I had zero career development skills. You gave me an opportunity to attend grad school by paying my tuition and giving me a stipend. Sure, this opportunity happens for lots of people, but for me, it was huge. I became the first person in my family to both graduate college and pursue a master's degree, and having assistance made earning a master's degree possible.

You gave me an incredible foundation for career development, helped me develop my teaching skills, and shared knowledge that still informs the way I approach life and work today. You didn't fire me when I made mistakes or lost focus – you helped redirect me. This experience has made me a better professional, and a better person, and I have gone on to share these skills and experiences with dozens of students and mentees.

If all that wasn't enough, you gave me the opportunity to pursue my first college teaching job, and showed me what can happen when you bring awesome people together to work on a shared vision. I learned the importance of working with people you enjoy and respect, and even enjoyed one of those people so much that I ended up marrying them!

IU, you gave me so much.

ESPN, *X-Games Event Development Staff,* age 24

You made five year old Megan's dream of working for ESPN come true. You gave me the honor and privilege of working for an amazing company who organizes world class events. For the first time ever, I was rewarded financially for going above and beyond in my work. You invited me back year after year, giving me more responsibilities, and helping me learn all aspects of organizing and facilitating large scale events and managing sponsor development. You gave me the opportunity to meet Shawn White right after he landed the first perfect score in X-Games history, deliver a love note for Luis Vito, be a part of "Real World – Aspen", wear a real X-Games gold medal, ride the world's largest skateboard, emcee multiple Guinness world record competitions, and you introduced me to the world of action sports, giving me a front row view to watch AMAZING athletes compete at and complete unbelievable things. You also taught me that with the right people and leadership, strangers can come together and execute tasks at the highest level, working together to turn chaos into a beautifully designed VIP suite or interactive skate park. Thank you for one of the BEST EXPERIENCES of my life; I will NEVER forget the years I spent with all of you.

University of Iowa, *Assistant Director Career Leadership Academy & Career Advisor*, age 25

Even though I was right out of grad school, you created a dream position for me that I could never have imagined. Through the Career Leadership Academy, you allowed me to continue fostering my passions for career and leadership development, dramatically increasing my knowledge and skills in both areas, all while continuing to teach.

You allowed me to run wild with ideas. You listened to my advice when I said we needed more technology; you helped me build marketing skills by allowing me to manage social media, marketing, and branding projects even though they weren't in my job description and were outside of my area of expertise; and you paid for my Gallup Strengths certifications – a priceless gift that I will always be thankful for.

You showed me how fun work is when you love what you do and enjoy the people you work with.

You threw me the best going away party – one that communicated I was really a part of a supportive community – and you always smile when I return to visit. It was because of the experience I gained here that I was able to land my next dream job even though they were seeking somebody with five years' experience and a PhD – two things I definitely didn't have.

University of Wisconsin-Madison – School of Human Ecology, *Faculty Associate and Coordinator of Career and Leadership Services*, age 27

You took a chance on me! You gave me the opportunity to create a career and leadership center from the ground up, an accomplishment I thought was at least ten years down the road for me. You hired me in as a Faculty Associate, which was pretty much the coolest role I could ever have imagined, with the longest title of any job I've had to date.

You gave me the opportunity to co-chair a Career & Leadership Task Force where we developed unique innovative approaches to help lead and develop students, and I'm still proud of the model we created.

You also put me on the Virtual Brand Task Force, where I had an active role in the school's complete website re-design, allowing me to work with an incredible branding team and marketing agency.

You allowed me to create a peer career advisor program, a celebration event for students, faculty, and staff, and even stretched my teaching capacity from classes of 20-30 to 120.

Finally, you introduced me to 'Design Thinking', a skill I still find myself using every day!

ILC, *VP of Innovation and Strategy*, age 28

You gave me the opportunity to make a pitch to a room full of millionaires about why they should hire me, and offered my first full time professional experience in the world of entrepreneurship. You then told me to choose my own title, and gave me the kind of responsibilities that helped me learn and grow in ways I couldn't have imagined.

Working for you, I was able to learn about building company culture, a skill that would become invaluable in ways I could never have imagined. Through this experience, I gained the courage to leave the stability of higher education to work for a startup, and eventually led to me fulfilling a huge ***Someday Goal*** – opening my own business.

I just can't thank you enough.

PRACTICING GRATITUDE

ACKNOWLEDGEMENTS

*For all of the people who helped me in my **Discover.** phase:*

To Mama Watt – you technically get the most credit for helping me get this book done, because without you, I wouldn't even exist! On a more serious note, thank you for offering me unconditional love from the very beginning. Your love and support have been the foundation of who I am today, all that I've done, and all that I will do. This foundation has been the key to my self confidence and my success. Thank you for being my mom! I love you more!!

To Grammy & Grandpa (Patricia & John Watt) – you are the best grandparents in the world. You always made me feel special and loved, and you spoiled me just the way grandparents should. You taught me the importance of fun, laughter, determination, passion, and being involved. I know you're smiling down on me now, beaming from ear to ear that your 'little genius' finally likes reading, and, believe it or not, has even written a book! I love you forever.

To my "adoptive parents" – the tribe members of the village who helped raise me" – thank you for all of the time, love, and lessons you taught me as I grew up. I am forever grateful and will always be indebted to you…

Much love to you: MaryAnn DiNella & Jeannie DiNella-McCormick, Barbara & Hank Neumann, Suzanne & Jake Miller, Janet & Tom O., Bari & Ron Litschauer, Barb & Troy Moore, Patty & Hootie Coats,

Rochelle & Norm Morris, Ernie Williams, June & Larry Boresma, and Jeannie & Sam Ferguson.

To David Pittman and Laura Osteen – thank you for being the #1 mentors of ALL time (I'll let you two duke it out for ranking). You both have helped shape me into the person I am today, and I am so incredibly grateful you both have stayed a part of my life. You provide me the perfect balance of challenge and support, with a whole LOT of FUN mixed in there. I love you tons.

To Vinny Bocchino – You hired me for the Dance Marathon Overall Committee even when I had no experience or skills to actually be the Technology Chair. I put you on a pedestal when I first saw you on stage way back when in the DM polo.

When I finally met you and got to see you in full action, and briefly got to work with you, you lived up to your place on that pedestal. For the next three years while I served on the DM overall committee, I always asked myself WWVD (what would Vinny do) whenever I had any doubts. When I finally passed on the Overall Director reigns, I was so proud because I had left DM better than I had found it, which I was only able to do with your guidance. I know I made you proud with all of the ways we grew. My work with DM was a ***Catalyst Move*** that led to my first career in Student Affairs and then to my second career as a speaker and coach. Just two months after I started my business full time, I got to speak at the 15th Anniversary of DM at FSU, and saw them break the Million-dollar mark. I had a flood of memories of my first DM when I saw you on stage and y'all had just broken the $200,000 mark. Things have come a long way. While you were not able to be there for that moment, and hear the full impact of your life on mine, I proudly shared it with 1000+ DM dancers, and your family while sporting my Team Vinny shirt. We formed the first ever alumni team in your honor, raised over $21,000 and even won our division. Vinny, you are forever in my heart; I miss you friend. #FTK

*For all of the people who helped me in my **Act.** phase:*

To Ilsa – you are the best thing that has ever happened to me, and you are the most beautiful person inside and out. Every day, waking up as your wife is a gift. Ilsa, I love you to the moon and back.

To Nick – you deserve a LOT of the credit for getting this book started and completed. Thank you for believing in me and constantly providing me new opportunities to grow and learn. You pushed me to do this book on multiple occasions, and it probably would have been several years for me to complete something like this…seriously…if it hadn't been for your support.

To Danielle, Vasti, TNL and any other grad school professor of mine – thank you for all of the really long papers you made me write during my time at IU. Without knowing it, you taught me the power of a deadline and how that can help you get the necessary creative juices flowing to overcome 'writer's block'. Also, thanks for all of the other 'stuff' you taught me about life and higher education. I am a better, smarter, and more inclusive person because it.

To Megan Palmer – you were my #1 cheerleader during grad school at IU! I'm especially thankful for the number of times you motivated me, and sometimes, even yelled, when necessary. I'm so grateful for ALL of the other 'developmental' and 'not-so-developmental' talks we have had over the years.

To Beth Kreitl, Katie Lloyd, Kelley Ashby, and Stacy Narcotta-Welp – thank you for hiring me! My jobs at Indiana & Iowa taught me at least half of what I know about career and leadership development, supervision, professionalism, excellence, hard work, leading by example, compassion, and being an all-around awesome person who uses that awesomeness to do good. You will NEVER truly know how much you have impacted my life, how grateful I am to have had the chance to work with and to learn from you, and how often I think of you and the things you taught me.

To Mike Greeby – you are absolutely one of the most inspiring people I know. I love how much we encourage and push each other to take things to the next level. For years you were the grasshopper and I was the teacher, and now our roles have switched (at least sometimes). Thank you for being an amazing friend. Here's to M&M and *Crushing It*!

To Chris Rudolph – you are the ultimate Connector, and I'm so glad you are on my Dream Team. Since the day of our random meeting, you have been the single GREATEST catalyst for helping me accomplish my latest dream jobs and making progress on my ***Someday Goals***. Thank you for being an amazing friend and supporter by providing me opportunities to do what I love, and by making professional introductions.

To the DreamBank (the staff and visitors) – you are the second most magical place on earth! And you're only second to Disney World, so that's pretty impressive! Thank you for providing a beautiful and inspiring place for people to build and pursue their dreams. I've said it before, but I'll say it again – "The DreamBank changed my life. It's that simple."

To American Family Insurance, Michelle Post and the AmFam Women's Business Resource Group – thank you for hiring me to do the first ever *Discover. Act. Engage.* program. It was called something else at the time, but preparing and delivering that program was the most exciting work I had ever done. When the program finished, I knew immediately that I was doing what I was 'meant' to be doing.

Discover. Act. Engage.

The hundreds of pieces of positive feedback I received validated my feelings and helped urge me on. Thank you for being at the origin of *Discover. Act. Engage.* I am forever grateful.

To UpStart (staff, instructors, and participants) – you gave me a foundation for being an entrepreneur and running a business. The people I've met and everything I learned while in UpStart has completely transformed my "business" into a real business. Thank you for everything!

To Hal Elrod – thank you for the gift of *The Miracle Morning*. It has completely changed my life. I never thought I would enjoy waking up at 5:30am every morning. Because of you and *The Miracle Morning*, I am happier, healthier, and more productive. Working with you and learning from you has helped me 10X my life and see an entire new world of possibilities. Thank you!

*For all of the people who helped me in my **Engage.** phase:*

To my in-laws Barb, Mike, Bo, Briony, Pearl, Alex (and Darwin) – I am incredibly grateful and proud to be a part of your family. Thank you for welcoming me and supporting me from day one. I love you!

To everyone who supported me during the writing, editing, and promotion of this book – none of you ever laughed at me when I randomly texted or emailed you about this project, even when I told you I was trying to do it in a week. Thank you for providing excellent feedback and ideas throughout the process, and most of all, thank you for being amazing friends and supporters…

I love you all: Anna, Haley, Jen, Kristen, Kaylee, Kelly, Lisa, Sam, Sarah, Mike, Yabs, Dane, Abbie, Bo, Susan, Spencer, Rebecca, Kellie, and to those I may have missed, please know there was not a single

Facebook like, comment, or other message that went unnoticed – they meant the world to me when I put it out there into the universe that I was writing a book.

To Adam Carroll – you are my #1 Industry Insider. You encouraged me to embrace being "Mega Watt" and that I could be a successful entrepreneur and speaker. You helped me accomplish a bucket list item when you invited me to jump out of a plane. I always joked, "we were ten years apart in life and in business," and then recently I found out we really are almost to the day. Go Virgos! Keep blazing ahead so I can follow your lead and continue to learn from you. Thank you for all of your time and support over the years.

To Keith Nord – you are my #1 Momentum Mover. Never in a million years did I think I would be friends with a professional NFL player, let alone one who would take me under his wing and mentor me as I grew my speaking business. You are an excellent speaker and family man, who models the way for me. Thank you for setting such a wonderful example, and thank you for all of the wisdom you share with me during our talks. I am forever grateful for our friendship and your continued support.

To Darin Eich – you provided me with the *next right move* when I was looking to officially go out on my own and run Dream Catalyst Labs full time. You taught me a TON about business, technology, innovation, speaking, and facilitating. You will never know how much our friendship means to me and how grateful I was for the opportunity you gave me back in December 2014. Thank you!

To Jaime Tardy & Joel Louis – you have helped me double my business and provided me with an amazing community of awesome entrepreneurs. Your advice and support has been a ***CATALYST MOVE*** for my business and me. Thank you for teaching me how to hustle! Jaime, let me officially declare that I will go from Hustlers to being on your show someday!!

To Kim & Jason Kotecki, and Mark LeBlanc – thank you for telling me that seeing Mark speak at the NSA-WI chapter meeting was a MUST-attend event even though I was leaving the next day for one of biggest talks of my life, and had not even packed. You were 100% right. Mark rocked it. Also, thank you for being amazing role models and serving as Industry Insiders on my Dream Team. Your influence has translated into both my business and personal life.

Mark, you have an amazing gift and message that has resonated with me from the moment your words hit my ears. You challenged the group to have a book written by the end of 2016, a goal that, at the time, I completely laughed at. I thought that books are great for some people and some speakers, but I don't need one, at least not now. But here I am, less than 2 months after hearing your message, and I'm thanking you at the end of my first book. You were right, and I can't wait to keep using all of the things you taught me that night. Thank you all for being wonderful role models of class and excellence to the speaking profession.

To my Mastermind mind group (Amy, Jen, Lysianne, and Tina) – thank you for being totally awesome women who invited me into their group and still provide me SO MUCH value and support. I'm grateful to know you, work with you, and now, to be able to call you friends.

To She Did It Her Way – you are making a difference in my life and in the world of entrepreneurship. There is a HUGE need for a platform that highlights and encourages women to be entrepreneurs, and you do it with excellence. Thank you for the opportunity to be part of the community and to help shape it!

To Ryan-Ashley Anderson – you ROCK! You are the greatest editor I have ever had! Even though you are also technically the only one, it's still true. Thank you for making this book a hundred times better without losing my voice, and thank you for not thinking I was nuts to write a book in a week! You helped me meet my deadline. #LifeSaver

Hugo Fernandez & the Just Digital Team – WOW!! That's all I can say. Y'all did an AMAZING job with the cover design of this book. You worked with very few ideas in the beginning, and then incorporated my feedback beautifully – it was all absolutely incredible. Your quality is top notch, and even though I'm a first time author, my book cover looks like that of a true professional's. Also, thank you for helping turn all this around in such a short time period.

Last, but certainly NOT LEAST...To YOU the reader! – thank you for taking a chance on me by picking up this book. I hope that you find at least one little nugget that inspires you to believe more deeply in yourself and your ***Someday Goals***, and I hope it inspires you to take action! I would love to hear how this book has impacted you in any way, big or small, so please reach out to me at **dreamcatalyst.org** or on social media to share.

Reader, DON'T EVER FORGET! YOU TOO CAN ACCOMPLISH YOUR ***SOMEDAY GOALS*** AND MAKE A DIFFERENCE IN THIS WORLD!

ABOUT DREAM CATALYST LABS

Dream Catalyst Labs (DCL) is on a mission to empower and inspire individuals and organizations to identify and pursue their dreams through speaking, training, and coaching. We believe that when you have self-confidence, know your purpose, and leverage your strengths, you can achieve your *Someday Goals*, positively impact your community, and create lasting change.

DCL started with family and friends asking for help finding a job, reviewing a resume, or preparing for an upcoming interview. Dream Catalyst Creators, Ilsa May and Megan Watt both participated in two years of training in Career Advising and teaching at Indiana University's Career Development Center before embarking on this journey. We realized that it's not only new professionals who need career advice, but individuals of all ages and walks of life, so we sought a path to formally offer our knowledge and expertise to those in need of help fulfilling their personal, professional, and educational goals.

What really motivated us to create and formalize Dream Catalyst Labs was our own career development experiences. Finding a dream job and doing what you love is attainable, and we hope to empower and assist people in achieving their dreams, whatever they are! Megan took over as Chief Dream Maker of DCL in January 2015 and it's been a wonderful wild rollercoaster ever since! We think of DCL as the catalyst to helping people achieve their *Someday Goals* through speaking, coaching, and training.

ABOUT THE AUTHOR

Megan Watt is a wife, dream catalyst, speaker, career coach, strengths & leadership geek, facilitator, FSU & IU Alum, AXO, and a lover of fun facts… quiz her if you want! One fun fact is that she's ridden the world's largest skateboard while working for ESPN's X-Games!

Megan is a highly sought after speaker, facilitator, and career coach who brings an innovative approach to her work. Participants leave her sessions, talks, and workshops excited to take new action in their lives. She speaks to colleges and universities, Fortune 500 companies, and associations across the nation, on the power of strengths and the *Power of Connections* in the pursuit of your ***Someday Goals***.

Megan has been recognized by the Urban League as a Trailblazer – an award that recognizes young professionals who are excelling in their respective fields and show leadership within their industry. Before starting her own company, she taught career & leadership development at 3 Big Ten universities, helped raise $2.4 million dollars for Children's Miracle Network, and served as the VP of Innovation & Strategy for a local startup, increasing sales by 300% in 6 months. When she's not leading Dream Catalyst Labs, you can find her serving as a Money Mentor for National Financial Educators, Project Manager for Your Podcast Guru, and as a Coach & Ambassador for She Did It Her Way. All three platforms align with Megan's mission of helping people achieve their ***Someday Goals!*** Megan lives in Madison, WI with her wife, Ilsa, and their cat, Oliver.

BOOK MEGAN TO SPEAK!

Book Megan to speak at your next event and she's guaranteed to help you deliver an AMAZING EVENT!

Her high impact, interactive sessions put participants on the edge of their seats, and her breakout sessions are standing room only. When attendees are asked what they thought of Megan's presentations, they use words like, "engaging," "relatable," "inspirational," "fun," and "actionable." There are very few speakers who can create engaging programs for ages ranging from 12 to 88. Megan is one of those speakers, and she delivers WOW every single time she gets up on stage.

What Event Planners Are Saying:

> "Megan did a fantastic job – it was one of our highest attended events. Megan is engaging and is a dynamic speaker, and we enjoyed working with her. She really spent a lot of time with our team listening to what our objectives were and customizing the presentation. I would definitely recommend pursuing her. I think she really related well to our employee audience and to the young adults who attended the session. We would have Megan back anytime."
>
> **Michele Post,** Co-Lead Women's Business Resource Group,
> American Family Insurance

For more info, visit dreamcatalyst.org

Made in the USA
Charleston, SC
31 October 2016